The Family

OPPOSING VIEWPOINTS®

OTHER BOOKS OF RELATED INTEREST

OPPOSING VIEWPOINTS SERIES

Abortion
Adoption
An Aging Population
American Values
America's Children
Child Abuse
Child Welfare
Homosexuality
Human Sexuality
Male / Female Roles
Teenage Pregnancy
Violence
Welfare
Work
Working Women

CURRENT CONTROVERSIES SERIES

Family Violence
Gay Rights
Marriage and Divorce
Reproductive Technologies
Violence Against Women

AT ISSUE SERIES

Child Sexual Abuse
Domestic Violence
Gay Marriage
Single-Parent Families
Welfare Reform

The Family

OPPOSING VIEWPOINTS®

David L. Bender, *Publisher*
Bruno Leone, *Executive Editor*
Brenda Stalcup, *Managing Editor*
Scott Barbour, *Senior Editor*
Mary E. Williams, *Book Editor*
Karin L. Swisher, *Assistant Editor*

OPPOSING
VIEWPOINTS®
SERIES

Greenhaven Press, Inc., San Diego, California

Cover photo: Dover Books

Library of Congress Cataloging-in-Publication Data

The Family : opposing viewpoints / Mary E. Williams, book editor;
    Karin L. Swisher, assistant editor.
        p.   cm. — (Opposing viewpoints series)
    Includes bibliographical references and index.
    ISBN 1-56510-669-5 (lib. bdg. : alk. paper). —
ISBN 1-56510-668-7 (pbk. : alk. paper)
    1. Family—United States. 2. Divorce—United States. 3. Family
policy—United States. 4. Adoption—Government policy—United
States. I. Williams, Mary E., 1960–   . II. Swisher, Karin, 1966–   .
III. Series: Opposing viewpoints series (Unnumbered)
HQ536.F3754 1998
306.85'0973—dc21   97-19211
                                                                         CIP

Greenhaven Press, Inc., P.O. Box 289009
San Diego, CA 92198-9009

"Congress shall make no law...abridging the freedom of speech, or of the press."

First Amendment to the U.S. Constitution

The basic foundation of our democracy is the First Amendment guarantee of freedom of expression. The Opposing Viewpoints Series is dedicated to the concept of this basic freedom and the idea that it is more important to practice it than to enshrine it.

CONTENTS

WHY CONSIDER OPPOSING VIEWPOINTS?

"The only way in which a human being can make some
approach to knowing the whole of a subject is by hearing
what can be said about it by persons of every variety of
opinion and studying all modes in which it can be looked
at by every character of mind. No wise man ever acquired
his wisdom in any mode but this."

John Stuart Mill

In our media-intensive culture it is not difficult to find differing
opinions. Thousands of newspapers and magazines and dozens
of radio and television talk shows resound with differing points
of view. The difficulty lies in deciding which opinion to agree
with and which "experts" seem the most credible. The more in-
undated we become with differing opinions and claims, the
more essential it is to hone critical reading and thinking skills to
evaluate these ideas. Opposing Viewpoints books address this
problem directly by presenting stimulating debates that can be
used to enhance and teach these skills. The varied opinions contained in each book examine many different aspects of a single
issue. While examining these conveniently edited opposing
views, readers can develop critical thinking skills such as the
ability to compare and contrast authors' credibility, facts, argu-
mentation styles, use of persuasive techniques, and other stylis-
tic tools. In short, the Opposing Viewpoints Series is an ideal
way to attain the higher-level thinking and reading skills so essential in a culture of diverse and contradictory opinions.

In addition to providing a tool for critical thinking, Opposing
Viewpoints books challenge readers to question their own
strongly held opinions and assumptions. Most people form their
opinions on the basis of upbringing, peer pressure, and personal, cultural, or professional bias. By reading carefully bal-
anced opposing views, readers must directly confront new ideas
as well as the opinions of those with whom they disagree. This
is not to simplistically argue that everyone who reads opposing
views will—or should—change his or her opinion. Instead, the
series enhances readers' understanding of their own views by
encouraging confrontation with opposing ideas. Careful examination of others' views can lead to the readers' understanding of
the logical inconsistencies in their own opinions, perspective on

why they hold an opinion, and the consideration of the possibility that their opinion requires further evaluation.

Evaluating Other Opinions

To ensure that this type of examination occurs, Opposing Viewpoints books present all types of opinions. Prominent spokespeople on different sides of each issue as well as well-known professionals from many disciplines challenge the reader. An additional goal of the series is to provide a forum for other, less known, or even unpopular viewpoints. The opinion of an ordinary person who has had to make the decision to cut off life support from a terminally ill relative, for example, may be just as valuable and provide just as much insight as a medical ethicist's professional opinion. The editors have two additional purposes in including these less known views. One, the editors encourage readers to respect others' opinions—even when not enhanced by professional credibility. It is only by reading or listening to and objectively evaluating others' ideas that one can determine whether they are worthy of consideration. Two, the inclusion of such viewpoints encourages the important critical thinking skill of objectively evaluating an author's credentials and bias. This evaluation will illuminate an author's reasons for taking a particular stance on an issue and will aid in readers' evaluation of the author's ideas.

As series editors of the Opposing Viewpoints Series, it is our hope that these books will give readers a deeper understanding of the issues debated and an appreciation of the complexity of even seemingly simple issues when good and honest people disagree. This awareness is particularly important in a democratic society such as ours in which people enter into public debate to determine the common good. Those with whom one disagrees should not be regarded as enemies but rather as people whose views deserve careful examination and may shed light on one's own.

Thomas Jefferson once said that "difference of opinion leads to inquiry, and inquiry to truth." Jefferson, a broadly educated man, argued that "if a nation expects to be ignorant and free . . . it expects what never was and never will be." As individuals and as a nation, it is imperative that we consider the opinions of others and examine them with skill and discernment. The Opposing Viewpoints Series is intended to help readers achieve this goal.

David L. Bender & Bruno Leone,
Series Editors

Greenhaven Press anthologies primarily consist of previously published material taken from a variety of sources, including periodicals, books, scholarly journals, newspapers, government documents, and position papers from private and public organizations. These original sources are often edited for length and to ensure their accessibility for a young adult audience. The anthology editors also change the original titles of these works in order to clearly present the main thesis of each viewpoint and to explicitly indicate the opinion presented in the viewpoint. These alterations are made in consideration of both the reading and comprehension levels of a young adult audience. Every effort is made to ensure that Greenhaven Press accurately reflects the original intent of the authors included in this anthology.

INTRODUCTION

"Americans believe 'parents having less time to spend with their families' is the single most important reason for the family's decline in our society."

—William R. Mattox Jr.

"[Many men and women] . . . place the happiness and well-being of the family before their individual desires or ambitions."

—Barbara Dafoe Whitehead

In recent years, numerous policymakers and social scientists have warned that the family is threatened by a variety of social trends. Although some commentators disagree with these warnings and maintain that such concern is unfounded, the current debate has been focused primarily on identifying which problems most endanger American families. For example, many maintain that laws making divorce easier to obtain have irrevocably damaged the traditional two-parent family. Others believe that nontraditional families—whether single-parent families, nonmarried couples, or families headed by same-sex partners—do not receive enough social or governmental support. Various experts claim that an increase in families headed by single mothers has led to an economic and moral crisis in America, while others argue that a changing economic climate has made life more difficult for the modern family. According to journalist E.J. Dionne, however, a majority of Americans agree that balancing work time and family needs has become one of the nation's most challenging problems. In a 1995 *Washington Post* article, Dionne notes that "the concerns that parents [have] are the trade-offs they have to make . . . between raising their living standards by earning more money or having more time with their children."

Many experts argue that American families are in crisis because most employees spend too much time at work. According to Harvard economics lecturer Juliet Schor, in comparison to the 1960s the average American employee has added about 160 hours of work to his or her yearly schedule. Companies' reductions in personnel in the 1980s and 1990s—referred to as "downsizing"—have led to increased workloads for remaining employees, Schor asserts, which means that about half of all American employees work more than 45 hours per week. She also notes that single parents and two-career couples spend as much time on the unpaid labor of household chores as they do at their paying jobs. Furthermore, Schor points out, many workers hold two or more jobs to make ends meet financially. This is especially true for women workers, she contends, who are frequently hired for part-time or temporary positions. Such workloads leave many Americans with very little time or energy to attend to children's needs and family relationships, Schor argues.

Arlie Hochschild, a University of California sociology professor, contends that employees themselves can contribute to this work-family dilemma. Many people work long hours to avoid unhappy or difficult family situations, she maintains. According to her research, some employees prefer longer work hours because it gives their lives structure and a sense of accomplishment that they do not find at home. "Personal lives are far more complicated. . . . By working hard we have an excuse for avoiding confusing personal situations," Hochschild asserts.

Whether the work-family dilemma stems from companies' longer work hours or from employees' avoidance of home life, many commentators agree that inadequate time for family is especially harmful for children. Schor points out that an increasing number of children and teenagers are unsupervised when not in school and therefore "are at much higher risk for things like drug and alcohol use, show declining performances in school, and have a much higher rate of stress and anger." Economist Sylvia Hewlett, author of *When the Bough Breaks: The Cost of Neglecting Our Children*, agrees that children are adversely affected by this lack of parental supervision. She argues that in comparison with previous generations, young people today are more likely to "commit suicide, need psychiatric help, suffer a severe eating disorder, bear a child out of wedlock, [and] be the victim of a violent crime."

However, many authorities disagree with Schor, Hochschild, and Hewlett about the severity of the work-family conflict. Economist Gary Burtless, for example, argues that work hours have not increased during the last half of the twentieth century: "Among working age adults free time is up, while time devoted to work (including commuting and housework) is down." He points out that faulty polling techniques have often resulted in unreliable statistics about the average American's workload. In truth, Burtless argues, men are devoting more time to household tasks and working fewer hours for pay, while women do an increasing amount of paid work and spend less time on household chores. Moreover, he maintains, technological innovations have reduced the time required for housework. The average workload has actually fallen more than five hours a week since 1950, Burtless concludes.

Other experts maintain that working parents benefit the family. Caryl Rivers and Rosalind C. Barnett, authors of *She Works, He Works: How Two-Income Families Are Happier, Healthier and Better Off*, contend that dual-earner families are more financially and emotionally stable than the traditional breadwinner-father and homemaker-mother family. They argue that parents who work full time devote as much time to their children as do couples in which one partner is not employed. Furthermore, they point out, mothers who work for pay generally have higher self-esteem and better physical and mental health than nonemployed mothers and therefore have a positive influence on their children. "Contrary to myth," state Barnett and Rivers, "[working parents] are coping well with their often-stressful lives. . . . They report warm relations with their children, and that their children are thriving."

In contrast to the argument that employees often use work to avoid family life, Barbara Dafoe Whitehead, a former research associate at the Institute for American Values, contends that many middle-income parents are actually lightening their workloads so that they can devote more time to their families. In her opinion, American culture is shifting from an emphasis on career and self-fulfillment to a "new familism"—a growing recognition of the importance of family life. In effect, she argues, "both parents give up something in their work lives in order to foster their family lives." This trend may enable Americans "to make life better for children," she concludes.

It is difficult to draw general conclusions about the work-family issue because so many variables come into play—including the amount of time parents spend at work, the availability and quality of child care, the family's particular structure and socioeconomic class, and the emotional and financial needs of children and adults. However, since most sources agree that the percentage of children with single or married parents working outside the home is still rising, the national debate about work and family is likely to continue. *The Family: Opposing Viewpoints* examines this topic as well as other controversies about the changing family in the following chapters: What Is the State of the Family? How Have Divorce Law Reforms Affected the Family? How Do Work-Related Policies Affect the Family? Which Adoption Policies Deserve Support? Which Values and Policies Most Benefit the Family? Probing these issues reveals the various forces that strain and shape the contemporary family.

CHAPTER 1

WHAT IS THE STATE OF THE FAMILY?

CHAPTER PREFACE

In the United States, the foundation of the family, as traditionally defined, is a lifelong marital union between a man and a woman. The traditional definition also holds that the ideal nuclear family consists of a working father and a mother who stays home to raise children. According to public policy consultant Charmaine Crouse Yoest, such a family should provide "the fertile ground from which children acquire the patterns, habits, lessons, and values that, in our increasingly interdependent society, affect us all." Yoest and other advocates of the traditional family assert that the high divorce rate and the rise of single-parent female-headed homes has undermined the traditional family and has created a social and moral crisis in American society. They argue that children raised in broken homes and in homes without fathers are more likely to be emotionally unstable and socially disruptive. In their opinion, the decline of the nuclear family has contributed to increasing levels of societal immorality and violence.

Some social scientists and commentators disagree with the conclusions of Yoest and her colleagues. Family studies professor Stephanie Coontz, for example, contends that the family has never existed in just one ideal form: "American families always have been diverse, and the male breadwinner–female homemaker, nuclear ideal that most people associate with 'the' traditional family has predominated for only a small portion of our history." Furthermore, Coontz asserts, history reveals that traditional as well as nontraditional families have been beset by economic, social, and moral crises. She maintains that family structure is neither the cause of nor the solution to these societal problems. Judith Stacey, author of *Brave New Families*, agrees with Coontz and adds that "further stigmatizing the increasing numbers who live in 'nontraditional' families will only add to their duress."

Whether or not the family is in decline has become a subject of heated debate. The authors in the following chapter present several opposing arguments on the state of the modern family.

> "We view with uneasiness the consequences of the deconstruction of the family in the United States and in other free nations of the world."

THE FAMILY IS IN DECLINE

Ralph Segalman and Alfred Himelson

In the following viewpoint, Ralph Segalman and Alfred Himelson argue that the family has deteriorated in modern society. In the past, they maintain, a stable family unit ensured that its members learned vital moral rules and economic skills that strengthened the larger community. However, the authors contend, liberal principles have challenged traditional norms and values and have weakened the modern family. This decline in the family, the authors conclude, has led to widespread social disorder and chaos that threatens the future of democratic societies. Segalman and Himelson are both professors emeriti of sociology at the California State University in Northridge.

As you read, consider the following questions:

1. Which types of families existed in the past, according to the authors?
2. In the authors' opinion, what kinds of families are currently experiencing serious breakdown?
3. In what ways have politicians contributed to the crisis in the family, according to Segalman and Himelson?

From Ralph Segalman and Alfred Himelson, "The Family: Past, Present, and Future," *St. Croix Review*, December 1994. Reprinted with permission of the publisher.

At long last there is an increasing interest in the importance of the family by scholars, politicians, and the general public. After a century of the diminishment of the family and an increase in the role of the state in many aspects of human affairs, there is a growing realization that something has gone wrong in modern and transitional societies. The new interest may be connected with the deterioration of the family everywhere.

THE IMPORTANCE OF THE FAMILY

No matter what formal society (with the exception of such extreme varieties as Nazism or Communism, where the state dominates all), the family is the most important element in achieving and maintaining a society or civilization. The family is an important agent of socialization and almost always a necessary prerequisite to the individual's bond with larger society.

In the modernizing world, the maintenance and movement towards democracy cannot proceed unless people are adequately attached to the symbols, meanings, and morality of the political and social system. Unless there is learning within the family that the individual should be and can be a part of the larger society, the probability of the development of democracy with its advocacy of both competition and cooperation is diminished. The connection between the health of a democratic society and the state of the family has been largely minimized.

Much has been made in recent times of the search for happiness, and this has often been linked to finding "meaning-in-life." The ability to achieve this state of happiness and meaning has often been tied to individual development, but what has been ignored is that for the bulk of people, the family is the environment which provides the necessary prerequisites for later individual development, without which happiness is precluded.

A HISTORY OF THE FAMILY

In the past, societies were predominately rural in nature, and the bulk of the population lived off agriculture and handicraft. In some parts of the world the families were or are of the extended nature, that is, the authority and socialization system was larger than the mother/father/nuclear system. In other locations the families were largely nuclear (mother/father/children, plus perhaps some aged or handicapped relatives).

In either case, the family was crucial in developing in its children economically useful skills, such as to cooperate and minimize conflict within the family and the community, to ensure the continuation of a particular family and group, and to establish a proper relation with the religion(s). In these societies children were taught moral rules, proper roles, and necessary skills by a combination of formal education, role taking, and role playing. To assure that this learning took place, it was reinforced by the provision of a reward system of various rites of passage, and, if all else failed, through fear of ostracization or exile. The threat of exile was a life and death matter in earlier times.

With the threefold process of modernization, which included industrialization, urbanization, and political centralization, the family and its members found themselves in a different and often more difficult environment in that they were likely to be living among strangers (at least at the beginning) and under strange economic conditions and rules. But the institution of the family survived this often chaotic period, and the family as an institution was recognized as an important part of nation building, economic development, and security. There have been unintended consequences of modernization which weakened the family, but until very recent times there was no real attempt to *deliberately* weaken the family, or to downgrade it. . . .

There are two general categories of families which are experiencing serious crisis in modernized society. The first category is made up of families of affluence, and the second is made up of what we are calling the "distressed population."

The Children of the Affluent

In the first category, the children of the affluent (affluent is a relative term) were probably for the first time able to live by the libertarian standards which had their roots in the 19th century and had been given legitimacy in certain post–World War II liberal doctrines. This took concrete form in attacks on established authority, intolerance toward democratic institutions, assaults on concepts of competitive capitalism, and perhaps most important, in the long run, an attack on the very legitimacy of the family. Those holding these views no longer felt themselves bound by the constraints with which family membership is associated. Such previously disapproved behaviors as drug use, sexual promiscuity, social parasitism, etc., were now adopted as acceptable by sizable numbers of children of the affluent.

This challenge to the established norms and values has happened many times before in history. What made this situation so much more important than previous episodes of this kind was that it affected many more people because of the larger population who were now affluent, and also because this type of behavior was now blatant.

CHALLENGES TO THE FAMILY

Parallel and related to this was the nature of contemporary social science writings about the family. These often challenged the legitimate basis for the family and they themselves offered, under the disguise of a neutral social science, an advocacy of alternative lifestyles.

The irony of the attacks on the concept of the family is that even members of families become confused about whether their time-tested ways of doing things are legitimate and effective, and this confusion and uncertainty is passed on to the children.

THE BRADY BUNCH (1990's)*

Ramirez. Reprinted by permission of Copley News Service.

Another development which challenged the older concept of the family was the growth of some varieties of feminism (again, this was made possible by the economic affluence of the time). Members of these movements challenged the necessity of the intact family for child rearing and happiness.

A large body of empirical research has accumulated which shows the destructive consequences of the weakening of the family.

DISTRESSED POPULATIONS

Most modernized countries, and especially the United States, have a large permanent underclass of people who live very different family lives than most of the rest of the society. Theirs is a lifestyle that to some degree can be characterized by Oscar Lewis' *Culture of Poverty*, but with the significant difference that many of these people are regularly provided funds by the government. The mother, usually unmarried or divorced, is the receiver of these government funds, and men live outside regular permanent and family relationships. The next generation of children from such families often reproduces the same kind of family constellation when they have children (often in their teens).

There is an irony in comparing the family characteristics of these distressed families with those of affluent families. More and more they are beginning to resemble each other in terms of the percentage of children born outside of marriage, rates of destructive deviance (e.g., drug use, suicide rates, sexually transmitted diseases, etc.), plus sizable numbers of unemployables.

A sizable body of research has accumulated that illuminates the nature and dimensions of this social breakdown. . . .

SOCIETAL DYSFUNCTION

There are a number of conclusions that can be drawn from contemporary writings and research on the family.

The lack of effective family life is one major cause in the creation of a dysfunctional society. This is true in any of the phases of modernization, whether it be in North or South America, Africa, Europe, or Asia. Family life appears to be the major element in the creation of what Émile Durkheim called "social solidarity," where people are positively connected to each other.

Social pathologies are more likely to occur when people are not attached. In this view the family as an institution is not the oppressive monster that some modern sociologists have described. For example, recent empirical evidence has shown that children raised in single-parent or "reconstituted" families are more likely to have conflict within themselves, with others, and to violate the rules and responsibilities of the society.

GOVERNMENT INTRUSION

One principal agent which has weakened the functioning of the family is paradoxically one that was intended to ameliorate the difficulties experienced by individuals in modern society. This is the intrusion of government into what had formerly been the private affairs of family and neighborhood. While on the one hand the society sanctioned greater individual freedoms, on the other hand it increasingly has taken away power and authority from parents over their children. In the course of this happening, parents ceded many of their responsibilities to the "all-knowing" state. The further away from the family the power resides the more likely it is to create and compound negative unintended consequences. As one social philosopher described this process, it was done "with the best of intentions and the worst of results."

William J. Bennett has noted that "government, obviously, cannot fill a child's emotional needs. Nor can it fill his spiritual and moral needs. Government is neither a father nor mother. Government has never raised a child, and it never will." As James Q. Wilson put it, "Public interest depends on private virtue."

Presently many nations are experiencing a diminishment of private virtue. How can this be explained? Much of the world is more affluent today than beyond the wildest fantasies held by people a century ago. Our physical well-being, our material well-being, our political rights, and social and economic opportunities available to the average person are abundant. And yet, what we observe in the unvirtuous behavior of people living in these societies gives us cause for deep concern. Much of this result comes from failure in the family, or more drastically, in the lack of a family.

THE EFFECTS OF FAMILY DECLINE

The failure of effective family socialization makes for an unruly, unprepared, incompetent, and ineducable and unproductive population. It results in untrainable, technologically incapable people reflective of Sean O'Casey's comment that "all the world's a stage and all of us are actors, but too many of us are too bloody under-rehearsed" (to play our roles adequately in an increasingly complex civilized society).

Despite all the rhetoric by politicians about the crisis in the family, they appear to be making no effort to reduce the damage caused by the invasion of the monolithic government on the family and neighborhood. In fact, the intrusiveness is increasing.

When a public official speaks about safe sex to youth or discusses sex outside of marriage from a position of moral neutrality, children learn the lesson that sexual intercourse is okay even for teenagers. When a government agency or committee acknowledges or legalizes or recognizes anti-family behaviors, including non-marriage coupling, these actions serve to deconstruct the family. Such government involvement diminishes and devalues the normative family and its social relationships. Thus, out of one side of their mouth, representatives of government talk about the importance of the family and what is appropriate behavior within the family; but out of the other side of their mouth these same officials promote behavior which is obviously destructive to family life.

The economics and social life of modernized countries are more likely to become stagnant with a decline in the social health of the family. The first stage in producing competent individuals within the society is adequate socialization within the family. What is the content of this socialization? Respect for others; control of self; a sense of responsibility to others; an attachment to the positive symbols of the society; a valid sense of confidence in one's abilities and limits; and to some degree, a feeling of mastery over the immediate environment. If the family is absent, fragmented, dysfunctional, or powerless, then the socialization of its children will lead to weak, ineffectual, parasitic, or antisocial adults. This kind of society will be plagued by breakdowns in law and order. A belief that the government should take care of people no matter how they behave or live is certain to lead to dismal results either in the economic or social system or both.

THE THREAT TO COMMUNITIES

Daniel P. Moynihan, in his prophetic comments in 1965, warned that, "there is one unmistakable lesson in American history: a community that allows a large number of young men to grow up in broken families, dominated by women, never acquiring any stable relationship to male authority, never acquiring any set of rational expectations about the future—that community asks for and gets chaos. Crime, violence, unrest, disorder—most particularly, the furious, unrestrained lashing out at the whole social structure—that is not only to be expected: it is richly deserved." Moynihan's prophecy applies not only to the United States, but also to many other countries.

The presence of the malaise which Moynihan discusses is indicated by the enormous rate of marriage breakups, too-early "coupling," failed parent performances, weak and self-defeating mating practices, and an inability [for people] to function as [mature adults].

We note a variety of evidence of this malaise: rejection of responsibility and reasonable authority, excessive personal subjectivity, inability to distinguish between "feeling" and "thinking," reluctance to commit oneself while demanding the benefits of a social contract, i.e., wanting to "eat one's cake and have it," and not understanding why one cannot. [We see] a lack of understanding of role responsibility, role identity, let alone the values and skills related to the appropriate roles required for the benefits sought. We also observe an excessive atmosphere of "neurotic exemption," an avoidance of any thought or concern for consequences of one's behavior. We also note a pervasive atmosphere of "existential nausea," a condition in earlier times generally found only among the children of the rich but now increasingly prevalent among the children of the middle class. Further, it is also found among much of the welfare poor who have undertaken no commitments, who see no need for them, and who have run out of sufficiently thrilling experiences at their current level of gratification.

Societies in these positions of seeking to deal with adults who have not been adequately reared as children require other adults equipped with parent-like controls—controls powerful enough for the rehabilitation of so many of these adult adolescents—many of whom are stronger and more energetic than the shrinking pool of mature adults in their midst.

We view with uneasiness the consequences of the deconstruction of the family in the United States and in other free nations of the world. We fear for the fragile spirit of democracy because we believe that while healthy families can develop in many different kinds of political systems—one of the necessary conditions for the existence of a democratic society over time is the prevalence of a strong traditional family.

> "There is a positive new diversity springing up in families and relationships today in Western society."

NEW FAMILY FORMS ARE EMERGING

Shere Hite

Democracy is creating healthy changes in the family, argues Shere Hite in the following viewpoint. For much of history, she maintains, the typical family has been patriarchal—structured on a belief in male authority, female weakness, and children's obedience. In Hite's opinion, the patriarchal family is harmful because it forces men, women, and children to conform to limited roles based on female submission and acquiescence to male power. However, Hite contends, during the twentieth century, an emphasis on equality and justice has allowed nonpatriarchal families to emerge. This new diversity in families could lead to the development of a more egalitarian society, she concludes. Hite, a social researcher, is the author of *The Hite Report on the Family: Growing Up Under Patriarchy*.

As you read, consider the following questions:

1. According to Hite, why was the modern patriarchal family created?
2. Why is the idea of being loved confusing to children, in the author's opinion?
3. What are the effects of single-parent families on children, according to Hite?

Love and anger, love and obedience, love and power, love and hate. These are all present in family relationships. It's easy to say that they are inevitable, that stresses and strains are unavoidable, given "human nature." To some extent this is true, but these stresses and strains are exaggerated by a tense and difficult family system that is imposed upon our emotions and our lives, structuring them to fit its own specified goals.

Is the family as we have known it for so long the only way to create safe, loving, and caring environments for people? The best way? To understand the family in Western tradition, we must remember that much of what we see, say, and think about it is based on the archetypal family that is so pervasive in our society—Jesus, Mary, and Joseph. There is no daughter icon. This is the "holy family" model that we are expected, in one way or another, to live up to. But is this model really the right one for people who believe in equality and justice? Does it teach a good understanding of love and the way to make relationships work when we become adults?

One constantly hears that the family is in trouble, that it doesn't work anymore, that we must find ways to help it. If the family doesn't work, maybe there is something wrong with its structure. People must have reasons for fleeing the nuclear family: human rights abuses and the battering of women are well documented in many governments' statistics.

THE "DEMOCRATIZED" FAMILY

The family is changing because only in recent decades has the process of democratization, which began in Western political life more than two centuries ago, reached private life. Although John Stuart Mill wrote in favor of women's rights in the egalitarian democratic theory he helped develop, the family and women's role in the world were left out of most discussions of democracy, left in the "sacred" religious domain. Women and non-property owners, as well as "minorities," did not have the vote when democracy first began. Men made a fatal mistake. The democracy they thought they could make work in the public sphere would not really work without democracy in private life.

Some people, of course, are alarmed by changes in the family. Reactionary fundamentalist groups have gone on the offensive to try to stop this process. Yet most people are happier with their personal lives today than people were 50 years ago. Women especially have more choices and freedom than they did in the past. There is a positive new diversity springing up in families and relationships today in Western society. This pluralism should be valued and encouraged: far from signaling a breakdown of society, it is a sign of a new, more open and tolerant society springing up, a new world being born out of the clutter of the old.

DIVERSE FAMILIES OFFER HEALTHY POSSIBILITIES

Democracy could work even better if we changed the aggressive personality that is being created by the patriarchal family system. Children brought up with choice about whether to accept their parents' power are more likely to be confident about believing in themselves and their own ideas, less docile or habituated to bending to power. Such a population would create and participate in public debate very differently. And there are many more advances we are on the threshold of achieving: naming and eliminating emotional violence, redefining love and friendship, progressing in the areas of children's rights and in men's questioning of their own lives.

My work salutes the gentler and more diverse families that seem to be arising. They are part of a system that does not keep its members in terror: fathers in terror lest they not be "manly" and able to support it all; mothers in terror lest they be beaten in their own bedrooms and ridiculed by their children; children in terror of being forced to do things against their will and having absolutely no recourse, no door open to them for exit.

A NEW THEORY OF THE FAMILY

What I am offering is a new interpretation of relationships between parents and children, a new theory of the family. My interpretation of the data from my questionnaires [given to more than 3,000 people primarily from Western nations] takes into account not only the individual's unique experiences, as is done in psychology, but also the cultural backdrop—the canvas of social "approval" or "disapproval" against which children's lives are lived. This interdisciplinary theory also takes into account the historical ideology of the family; those who took part in my research are living in a world where perception of "family" is filtered through the Christian model of the "holy family" with its reproductive icons of Jesus, Mary, and Joseph. But no matter how beautiful it appears (especially in its promise of "true love"), this family model is an essentially repressive one, teaching authoritarian psychological patterns, meekness in women, and a belief in the unchanging rightness of male power. In this hierarchical family, love and power are inextricably linked, a pattern that has damaging effects not only on all family members but on the politics of the wider society. How can there be successful democracy in public life if there is an authoritarian model in private life?

So used have we become to these symbols that we continue to believe—no matter what statistics we see in the newspapers about divorce, violence in the home, mental breakdown—that the icons and the system they represent are right, fair, and just. We assume without thinking that this model is the only "natural" form of family, and that if there are problems it must be the individual who is at fault, not the institution.

We need a new interpretation of what is going on. We may be at one of the most important turning points of the Western world, the creation of a new social base that will engender an advanced and improved democratic political structure.

THE PATRIARCHAL FAMILY

Creating new, more democratic families means taking a clear and rational look at our institutions. We tend to forget that the family was created in its current form in early patriarchy for political, not religious, reasons. The new political order had to solve a specific problem: How could lineage or inheritance flow through men (and not women as it had previously) if men do not bear children?

The modern patriarchal family was created so that each man would "own" a woman who would reproduce for him. He then had to control the sexuality of "his" woman, for how else could he be sure that "his" child was really his? Restrictions were placed on women's lives and bodies by men; women's imprisonment in marriage was made a virtue, for example, through the later archetype of the self-sacrificing Mary, who was happy to be of service, never standing up for herself or her own rights. Mary, it is important to note, is a later version of a much earlier Creation Mother goddess. In her earlier form, she had many more aspects, more like the Indian goddess Kali than the "mother" whom the Christian patriarchal system devised.

Fortunately, the family is a human institution: humans made it and humans can change it. My research indicates that the extreme aggression we see in society is not a characteristic of biological "human nature" (as Freud concluded), nor a result of hormones. "Human nature" is a psychological structure that is carefully implanted in our minds—for life—as we learn the love and power equations of the family. Power and love are combined in the family structure: in order to receive love, most children have to humiliate themselves, over and over again, before power.

In our society, parents have the complete legal, economic, and social "right" to control children's lives. Parents' exclusive power over children creates obedience. Children are likely to take on authoritarian emotional, psychological, and sexual patterns, and to see power as one of the central categories of existence.

THE NEED FOR FAMILY LOVE

Love is at the heart—so to speak—of our belief in the importance of the family. The desire for love is what keeps us returning to the icons. Even when they don't seem to work in our lives, we try and try again. We are told that we will never find love if we don't participate in the family. We hear repeatedly that the only place we will ever be able to get security, true acceptance, and understanding is in the family; that we should distrust other forms of family; that we are only "half a family" or a "pretend family" if we create any other human group; that without being a member of the family we will be forever "left out," lonely, or useless. No one would want to deny the importance of love, or of lasting relationships with other people. But the violent, distorted definitions of love created by the patriarchal family make it difficult for love to last, and to be as profound as it could be.

How confusing it is for children, the idea of being loved! They are so often told by their parents, "Of course we love you, why do you even ask?" It is easy for children to believe that the emotion they feel when faced with a powerful person is "love"—or that the inscrutable ways of a person who is sometimes caring and friendly, and other times punitive and angry, are loving. The problem then is that, since the parents are still the providers and "trainers" of the children, legally and economically the "owners" of the children, they exercise incredible power over the children—the very power of survival itself.

Children must feel gratitude, and so, in their minds, this gratitude is mixed with love. How much of the love they feel is really supplication before the power of the parents? How will they define love later in life? Won't they be highly confused by passion (either emotional or physical) and what it means, unable to connect it with other feelings of liking and concern? Of course, long-term caring for others is something positive that can also be learned in families, but it can be learned in other kinds of families, not just the nuclear model. . . .

SINGLE-PARENT FAMILIES

There are very few carefully controlled studies of the effects of single-parent families on children. Today, much popular journalism assumes that the two-parent family is better for children. My data show that there are beneficial effects for the majority of children living in single-parent families. It is more positive for children not to grow up in an atmosphere poisoned by gender inequality.

Do girls who grow up with "only" their mother have a better relationship with her? According to my study, 49 percent of such girls felt that it was a positive experience; 20 percent did not like it; and the rest had mixed feelings. Mothers in one-parent families are more likely to feel freer to confide in daughters because no "disloyalty to the spouse" is implied. Daughters in such families are less likely to see the mother as a "wimp"—she is an independent person.

WHEN PROMOTING FAMILY VALUES, DON'T FORGET TO SPECIFY WHICH FAMILY.

Lowe. Reprinted by permission: Tribune Media Services.

Boys who grow up with "only" their mother experience less pressure to demonstrate contempt for things "feminine" and for nonaggressive parts of themselves. In *The Hite Report on Men and Male Sexuality*, I was surprised to find that boys who grew up with their mother alone were much more likely to have good relationships with women in their adult lives: 80 percent of men from such families had formed strong, lasting ties with women (in marriage or long-term relationships), as opposed to only 40 percent from two-parent families. This does not mean that the two-parent family cannot be reformed so that it provides a peaceful environment for children—indeed this is part of the ongoing revolution in the family in which so many people today are engaged.

Single-parent families are mostly headed by mothers, yet there is an increasing number of single-father families. Many single fathers don't take much part in child care but instead hire female nannies or ask their mothers, sisters, or girlfriends to take care of the children. Men could change the style of families by taking more part domestically, and by opening up emotionally and having closer contact with children. My research highlights men's traumatizing and enforced split from women at puberty. Healing this is the single most important thing we as a society could do to bridge the distance men feel from "family."

A POSITIVE PLURALISM

If you listen to people talk about their families, it becomes clear that we must give up on the outdated notion that the only acceptable families are nuclear families. We should not see the new society that has evolved over the last 40 years as a disaster simply because it is not like the past.

The new diversity of families is part of a positive pluralism, part of a fundamental transition in the organization of society that calls for open-minded brainstorming by all of us: What do we believe "love" and "family" are? Can we accept that the many people fleeing the nuclear family are doing so for valid reasons? If reproduction is no longer the urgent priority that it was when societies were smaller, before industrialization took hold, then the revolt against the family is not surprising. Perhaps it was even historically inevitable. It is not that people don't want to build loving, family-style relationships, it is that they do not want to be forced to build them within one rigid, hierarchical, heterosexist, reproductive framework. Diversity in family forms can bring joy and enrichment to a society: new kinds of families can be the basis for a renaissance of spiritual dignity and creativity in political as well as personal life.

Continuing this process of bringing private life into an ethical and egalitarian frame of reference will give us the energy and moral will to maintain democracy in the larger political sphere. We can create a society with a new spirit and will—but politics will have to be transformed. We can use the interactive frame of reference most often found today in friendships between women. Diversity in families can form the basic infrastructure for a new and advanced type of political democracy to be created, imagined, developed—a system that suits the massive societies that communications technology today has made into one "global village."

Promoting Justice

One cannot exaggerate the importance of the current debate: there has been fascism in societies before; it could certainly emerge again, alongside fascism in the family. If we believe in the democratic, humanist ideals of the last 200 years, we have the right, almost the duty, to make our family system a more just one; to follow our democratic ideals and make a new, more inclusive network of private life that will reflect not a preordained patriarchal structure, but our belief in justice and equality for all—women, men, and children. Let's continue the transformation, believe in ourselves, and go forward with love instead of fear. In our private lives and in our public world, let's hail the future and make history.

"One way the family has become
weaker is that more and more
children are being raised in one-
parent families."

SINGLE PARENTHOOD HAS HARMED
THE FAMILY

James Q. Wilson

In the following viewpoint, James Q. Wilson argues that single-
parent families are bad for children. Children raised by unmarried or divorced mothers are more likely to have emotional
problems and engage in criminal behavior, he contends. Furthermore, Wilson asserts, many teenagers who become mothers
go on welfare and remain unmarried, and the children of these
mothers are even more likely to become antisocial and delinquent. Children need the stability and security provided by a
home with two responsible parents, Wilson maintains. Wilson is
the Collins Professor of Management and Public Policy at the
University of California in Los Angeles.

As you read, consider the following questions:

1. According to Wilson, what is the public's view on the
   contemporary family?
2. What percentage of children live in two-parent homes,
   according to the author?
3. What were the findings of the 1988 study conducted by the
   Department of Health and Human Services, according to
   Wilson?

From James Q. Wilson, "The Family Values Debate." Reprinted from Commentary, April
1993, by permission; all rights reserved.

There are two views about the contemporary American family, one held by the public and the other by policy elites. In his presidential campaign, Bill Clinton appeared to endorse the public's view. . . .

The public's view is this: the family is the place in which the most basic values are instilled in children. In recent years, however, these values have become less secure, in part because the family has become weaker and in part because rivals for its influence—notably television and movies—have gotten stronger. One way the family has become weaker is that more and more children are being raised in one-parent families, and often that one parent is a teenage girl. Another way is that parents, whether in one- or two-parent families, are spending less time with their children and are providing poorer discipline. Because family values are so important, political candidates should talk about them, though it is not clear that the government can do much about them. Overwhelmingly, Americans think that it is better for children if one parent stays home and does not work, even if that means having less money.

DEBATES ABOUT THE FAMILY

No such consensus is found among scholars or policy-makers. That in itself is revealing. Beliefs about families that most people regard as virtually self-evident are hotly disputed among people whose job it is to study or support families.

A good example of the elite argument began in the fall of 1992 on the front page of the *Washington Post*, where a reporter quoted certain social scientists as saying that the conventional two-parent family was not as important for the healthy development of children as was once supposed. This prompted David Popenoe, a professor at Rutgers who has written extensively on family issues, to publish in the *New York Times* an op-ed piece challenging the scholars cited in the *Post*. Popenoe asserted that "dozens" of studies had come to the opposite conclusion, and that the weight of the evidence "decisively" supported the view that two-parent families are better than single-parent families.

Decisively to him, perhaps, but not to others. Judith Stacey, another professor of sociology, responded in a letter to the *Times* that the value of a two-parent family was merely a "widely shared prejudice" not confirmed by empirical studies; Popenoe, she said, was trying to convert "misguided nostalgia for 'Ozzie-and-Harriet'-land into social-scientific truth." Arlene and Jerome Skolnick, two more professors, acknowledged that although Popenoe might be correct, saying so publicly would "needlessly stigmatize children raised in families that don't meet the 'Ozzie-and-Harriet' model." After all, the Skolnicks observed, a man raised outside that model had just been elected President of the United States.

ACADEMIC ARGUMENTS

The views of Stacey and the Skolnicks are by no means unrepresentative of academic thinking on this subject. Barbara Dafoe Whitehead recently surveyed the most prominent textbooks on marriage and the family. Here is my paraphrase of her summary of what she found [Whitehead does not endorse the views she compiled]:

> The life course is full of exciting options. These include living in a commune, having a group marriage, being a single parent, or living together. Marriage is one life-style choice, but before choosing it people weigh its costs and benefits against other options. Divorce is a part of the normal family cycle and is neither deviant nor tragic. Rather, it can serve as a foundation for individual renewal and new beginnings. Marriage itself should not be regarded as a special, privileged institution; on the contrary, it must catch up with the diverse, pluralistic society in which we live. For example, same-sex marriages often involve more sharing and equality than do heterosexual relationships. But even in the conventional family, the relationships between husband and wife need to be defined after carefully negotiating agreements that protect each person's separate interests and rights.

Many politicians and reporters echo these sentiments and carry the argument one step further. Not only do poor Ozzie and Harriet (surely the most maligned figures in the history of television) stand for nostalgic prejudice and stigmatizing error, they represent a kind of family that in fact scarcely exists. [Former] Congresswoman Pat Schroeder has been quoted as saying that only about 7 percent of all American families fit the Ozzie-and-Harriet model. Our daily newspapers frequently assert that most children will not grow up in a two-parent family. The message is clear: not only is the two-parent family not especially good for children, but fortunately it is also fast disappearing.

TWO-PARENT FAMILIES ARE COMMON

Yet whether or not the two-parent family is good for children, it is plainly false that this kind of family has become a historical relic. For while there has been a dramatic increase in the proportion of children, especially black children, who will spend some or even most of their youth in single-parent families, the vast majority of children—nationally, about 73 percent—live in a home with married parents. Today, the mothers in those families are more likely to work than once was the case, though most do not work full time. (I am old enough to remember that even Harriet worked, at least in real life. She was a singer.)

The proponents of the relic theory fail to use statistics accurately. The way they arrive at the discovery that only 7 percent of all families fit the Ozzie-and-Harriet model is by calculating what proportion of all families consists *exactly* of a father, mother, and two (not three or four) children and in which the mother never works, not even for two weeks during the year helping out with the Christmas rush at the post office.

The language in which the debate over two-parent families is carried on suggests that something more than scholarly uncertainty is at stake. If all we cared about were the effects of one-versus two-parent families on the lives of children, there would still be a debate, but it would not be conducted on op-ed pages in tones of barely controlled anger. Nor would it be couched in slogans about television characters or supported by misleading statistics.

THE ROLE OF WOMEN

What is at stake, of course, is the role of women. To defend the two-parent family is to defend, the critics worry, an institution in which the woman is subordinated to her husband, confined to domestic chores with no opportunity to pursue a career, and taught to indoctrinate her children with a belief in the rightness of this arrangement. To some critics, the woman here is not simply constrained, she is abused. The traditional family, in this view, is an arena in which men are free to hit, rape, and exploit women. To defend the traditional family is to defend sexism. And since single-parent families are disproportionately headed by black women, criticizing such families is not only sexist but racist.

Perhaps the most influential book on this subject to appear during the 1970's was *The Future of Marriage* by Jessie Bernard, a distinguished scholar. Widely reviewed, its central message was that the first order of business for marriage must be "mitigating its hazards for women."

Unlike more radical writers, Bernard thought that the future of marriage was assured, but this would be the case only because marriage would now take many forms. Traditional marriages would persist but other forms would gain (indeed, had already gained) favor—communes, group marriages, the *ménage à* trois, marital "swinging," unmarried cohabitation, and limited-commitment marriages. (She did not discuss mother-only families as one of these "options." Nor did she discuss race.) In principle, no one form was better than another because "there is nothing in human nature that favors one kind of marriage over another." In practice, the forms that were best were those that were best for the woman. What might be best for children was not discussed. Children, it would seem, were incidental to marriage, except insofar as their care imposed strains on their parents, especially their mothers.

CHILDREN IN ONE-PARENT HOMES

Children in one-parent families are six times likelier to be poor, according to the Census Bureau. They are two to three times likelier to have emotional and behavioral problems, according to the National Center for Health Statistics. They are likelier to drop out of high school, to get pregnant as teen-agers, to use drugs and to commit crimes.

Joseph Perkins, *San Diego Union-Tribune*, November 15, 1996.

The main theme of much of the writing about marriage and families during the 1970's and 1980's was that of individual rights. Just as polities were only legitimate when they respected individual rights, so also marriages were worthy of respect only when they were based on a recognition of rights.

This view impressed itself on many who were not scholars, as is evident from an essay published in 1973 in the *Harvard Educational Review*. It urged that the "legal status of infancy . . . be abolished" so that a child would be endowed with all the rights of an adult. Even more, any law that classified people as children and treated them differently from adults "should be considered suspect." As a result, the state "would no longer be able to assume the rationality of regulations based on age." The author of this essay was Hillary Rodham.

FAMILY STUDIES OF THE 1970's

A rights-based, individualistic view of marriage is questionable in its own terms, but these theoretical questions would become insuperable objections if it could be shown that children are harmed by growing up in mother-only, or communal, or swinging, or divorced households. The academic study of families during the 1970's, however, did not produce an unchallenged body of evidence demonstrating that this was the case. There were several studies that attempted to measure the impact of mother-only families on their children's school attainment, job success, and personal conduct, but many discovered either no effects or ones that were ambiguous or equivocal.

I first became aware of this in the early 1980's when Richard J. Herrnstein and I were writing *Crime and Human Nature*. One of my tasks was to prepare the first draft of the chapter on the effects on crime rates of what were then called broken homes. I fully expected to find a raft of studies showing that growing up in a mother-only home put the child, especially the boy, at risk for criminality.

I did not find what I had expected to find. To be sure, I ran across the familiar fact that men in prison tended disproportionately to come from broken homes, but men in prison also tended to have parents who were themselves criminal and to come from poor, minority backgrounds. Since these factors—class, race, parental criminality, and family status—tended to co-vary, it was not clear that family background had any effect independent of temperament or circumstance. Similarly, Elizabeth Herzog and Cecelia Sudia reviewed eighteen studies of female-headed families carried out between 1950 and 1970. They found that in seven there was more delinquency in father-absent homes, in four there was less, and in seven the results were mixed. Some studies showed boys in father-absent homes failing to develop an appropriate masculine identity and others uncovered no such effect. (There was—and is—ample evidence that children from cold, discordant homes are likely to have plenty of problems, but there are lots of cold, discordant two-parent families.)

SINGLE PARENTHOOD HARMS CHILDREN

Since I wrote that chapter, though, the evidence that single-parent families are bad for children has mounted. There will never be anything like conclusive proof of this proposition unless we randomly assign babies at birth to single- and two-parent families of various economic and ethnic circumstances and then watch them grow up. Happily the laws and customs of this country make such an experiment unlikely. Short of that, the best evidence comes from longitudinal studies that follow children as they grow up in whatever kind of family nature has provided.

One example: when the 5,000 children born in the United Kingdom during the first week of March 1946 were followed for three decades, those raised in families broken by divorce or desertion were more likely than those living in two-parent families to become delinquent.

A second example: for many years, Sheppard Kellam and his colleagues at Johns Hopkins University followed several hundred poor, black, first-grade children in a depressed neighborhood in Chicago. Each child lived in one of several different family types, depending on how many and what kinds of adults were present. In about one-third of families the mother was the only adult present; in another third there was both a mother and a father. (Only a tiny fraction was headed by a father with no mother present.) The remainder was made up of various combinations of mothers, grandparents, uncles, aunts, adult brothers and sisters, and various unrelated adults. By the time the children entered the third grade, those who lived with their mothers alone were the worst off in terms of their socialization. After ten years, the boys who had grown up in mother-only families (which by then made up about half the total) reported more delinquencies, regardless of family income, than those who had grown up in families with multiple adults, especially a father. . . .

The most recent important study of family structure was done in 1988 by the Department of Health and Human Services. It surveyed the family arrangements of more than 60,000 children living in households all over the country. Interviews were conducted in order to identify any childhood problems in health, schoolwork, and personal conduct. These results were tabulated according to the age, sex, and ethnicity of the child and the income and marital status of the parents.

The results were striking. At every income level save the very highest (over $50,000 per year), for both sexes and for whites, blacks, and Hispanics alike, children living with a never-married or a divorced mother were substantially worse off than those living in two-parent families. Compared to children living with both biological parents, children in single-parent families were twice as likely to have been expelled or suspended from school, to display emotional or behavioral problems, and to have problems with their peers; they were also much more likely to engage in antisocial behavior. These differences were about as wide in households earning over $35,000 a year as they were in those making less than $10,000.

BAD HOME ENVIRONMENTS

Charles Murray of the American Enterprise Institute has been looking at the people whose lives have been followed by the National Longitudinal Study of Youth (NLSY) since they were in high school (they are now in their late twenties or early thirties). The NLSY not only keeps careful records of the schooling, jobs, and income of these young adults, it also looks at the home environment in which they are raising any children they may have. These home observations rate emotional quality, parental involvement in child care, style of discipline, and the like. The homes, thus observed, can be ranked from best to worst.

Murray has compared the home environments with the economic status of the parents and the legal status of the child. The odds of the children living in the worst home environments were powerfully affected by two things: whether the parents were married when they had the baby and whether they were regular welfare recipients. The child of an unmarried woman who was a chronic welfare recipient had one chance in six of growing up in the worst—that is, emotionally the worst—environment. The child of a married woman who never went on welfare had only one chance in 42.

Being poor hurts children. Living in a rotten neighborhood hurts them. Having cold or neglectful parents certainly hurts them. But so also does being illegitimate and living on welfare. This is generally true for whites as well as blacks.

TEENAGE MOTHERS

And so also does being a teenage mother. For many years, Frank Furstenberg of the University of Pennsylvania and his colleagues have been following 300 teenage mothers living in Baltimore. What they have found supports the public's view. Teenage girls who have babies fare much worse than ones who postpone child-bearing, and this is true even among girls of the same socioeconomic background and academic aptitude. They are more likely to go on welfare, and less likely to enter into a stable marriage. The children of teenage mothers, compared with those of older ones, tend to have more trouble in school, to be more aggressive, and to have less self-control. This is especially true of boys.

We have always had teenage mothers, and in some less-developed societies that is the norm. What is new and troubling about the present situation is the vast increase in the number of teenage mothers and their concentration in the same neighborhoods. A girl with a baby presents one kind of problem when she is either a rarity or is embedded in an extended family that provides guidance and assistance from older women living with her. She presents a very different and much more serious problem when she is one of thousands of similarly situated youngsters living in the same neighborhood or public-housing project, trying to maintain an independent household on welfare. . . .

THE PUBLIC IS RIGHT

I think that the American people are right in their view of families. When they look at the dramatic increase in divorce, single-parent families, and illegitimate children that has taken place over the last 30 years, they see families in decline. They do not need studies to tell them that these outcomes are generally bad, because they have had these outcomes happen to them or to people they know. Divorce may sometimes be the right and necessary remedy for fundamentally flawed marriages and for the conditions created by an abusive or neglectful spouse, but in general divorce makes people worse off: the woman becomes poorer and the children more distressed. Properly raising a child is an enormous responsibility that often taxes the efforts and energies of two parents; one parent is likely to be overwhelmed. Children born out of wedlock are in the great majority of cases children born into poverty. Millions of people are living testimony to these bleak facts. If scholars say that the evidence is not conclusive, so much the worse for scholars. But now, I believe, scholars are starting to find hard facts to support popular impressions.

| "Celebrating marriage brings a renewed stigmatization of [single] women, and makes them scapegoats for social ills of which they are often the most serious victims."

SINGLE PARENTHOOD HAS BEEN UNFAIRLY STIGMATIZED

Iris Marion Young

Iris Marion Young is the author of *Justice and the Politics of Difference*. In the following viewpoint, Young takes issue with researchers and politicians who claim that only traditional two-parent families can raise children successfully. In Young's opinion, families headed by divorced and unmarried mothers are wrongly blamed for fostering poverty, juvenile delinquency, and other social ills. There is little conclusive evidence that single-parent families are harmful, Young contends. Instead of stigmatizing these families, society should give them the economic and social support they need, she argues.

As you read, consider the following questions:

1. In what ways are the data on children of divorce flawed, according to Young?
2. What kinds of discrimination do single mothers face, according to the author?
3. In Young's opinion, why do many teenage girls decide to bear children?

Excerpted from Iris Marion Young, "Making Single Motherhood Normal," Dissent, Winter 1994.

When Dan Quayle denounced Murphy Brown for having a baby without a husband in May 1992, most liberals and leftists recognized it for the ploy it was: a Republican attempt to win an election by an irrational appeal to "tradition" and "order." To their credit, American voters did not take the bait. The Clinton campaign successfully turned the family values rhetoric against the GOP by pointing to George Bush's veto of the Family and Medical Leave Act and by linking family well-being to economic prosperity.

Nonetheless, family values rhetoric survived the 1992 election. Particularly disturbing is the fact that the refrain has been joined by people who, by most measures, should be called liberals, but who can accept only the two-parent heterosexual family. Communitarians are leading the liberal chorus denouncing divorce and single motherhood. In The Spirit of Community, Amitai Etzioni calls for social measures to privilege two-parent families and encourage parents to take care of young children at home. Etzioni is joined by political theorist William Galston—White House adviser on domestic policy [from 1993 to 1995]—in supporting policies that will make divorce more difficult. Jean Bethke Elshtain is another example of a social liberal—that is, someone who believes in state regulation of business, redistributive economic policies, religious toleration and broad principles of free speech—who argues that not all kinds of families should be considered equal from the point of view of social policy or moral education. William Julius Wilson, another academic who has been close to Democratic party policy makers, considers out-of-wedlock birth to be a symptom of social pathology and promotes marriage as one solution to problems of urban black poverty.

SINGLE MOTHERS ARE SCAPEGOATS

Although those using family values rhetoric rarely mention gays and lesbians, this celebration of stable marriage is hardly good news for gay and lesbian efforts to win legitimacy for their lives and relationships. But I am concerned here with the implications of family values rhetoric for another despised and discriminated-against group: single mothers. Celebrating marriage brings a renewed stigmatization of these women, and makes them scapegoats for social ills of which they are often the most serious victims. The only antidote to this injustice is for public policy to regard single mothers as normal, and to give them the social supports they need to overcome disadvantage.

Most people have forgotten another explicit aim of Dan

Quayle's appeal to family values: to "explain" the disorders in Los Angeles in May 1992. Unmarried women with children lie at the source of the "lawless social anarchy" that sends youths into the streets with torches and guns. Their "welfare ethos" impedes individual efforts to move ahead in society.

Liberal family values rhetoric also finds the "breakdown" of "the family" to be a primary cause of all our social ills. "It is not an exaggeration," says Barbara Dafoe Whitehead in the *Atlantic* (April 1993) "to characterize [family disruption] as a central cause of many of our most vexing social problems, including poverty, crime, and declining school performance." Etzioni lays our worst social problems at the door of self-indulgent divorced or never-married parents. "Gang warfare in the streets, massive drug abuse, a poorly committed workforce, and a strong sense of entitlement and a weak sense of responsibility are, to a large extent, the product of poor parenting." Similarly, Galston attributes fearsome social consequences to divorce and single parenthood. "The consequences of family failure affect society at large. We all pay for systems of welfare, criminal justice, and incarceration, as well as for physical and mental disability; we are all made poorer by the inability or unwillingness of young adults to become contributing members of society; we all suffer if our society is unsafe and divided."

FAULTY ARGUMENTS

Reductionism in the physical sciences has faced such devastating criticism that few serious physicists would endorse a theory that traced a one-way causal relationship between the behavior of a particular sort of atom and, say, an earthquake. Real-world physical phenomena are understood to have many mutually conditioning forces. Yet here we have otherwise subtle and intelligent people putting forward the most absurd social reductionism. In this simplistic model of society, the family is the most basic unit, the first cause that is itself uncaused. Through that magical process called socialization, families cause the attitudes, dispositions, and capacities of individual children who in turn as adults cause political and economic institutions to work or not work.

The great and dangerous fallacy in this imagery, of course, is its implicit assumption that non-familial social processes do not cause family conditions. How do single-mother families "cause" poverty, for example? Any sensible look at some of these families shows us that poverty is a cause of their difficulties and failures. Doesn't it make sense to trace some of the conflicts that motivate divorce to the structure of work or to the lack of work? And what about all the causal influences on families and children over which parents have very little control—peer groups, dilapidated and understaffed schools, consumer culture, television and movie imagery, lack of investment in neighborhoods, cutbacks in public services? Families unprotected by wide networks of supportive institutions and economic resources are bound to suffer. Ignoring the myriad social conditions that affect families only enables the government and the public to escape responsibility for investing in the ghettos, building new houses and schools, and creating the millions of decent jobs that we need to restore millions of people to dignity.

Family-values reductionism scapegoats parents, and especially single parents, and proposes a low-cost answer to crime, poverty, and unemployment: get married and stay married.

DOES DIVORCE HARM CHILDREN?

Whitehead, Galston, Etzioni, and others claim that there is enough impressive evidence that divorce harms children emotionally to justify policies that discourage parents from divorcing. A closer look at the data, however, yields a much more ambiguous picture. One meta-analysis of ninety-two studies of the effects of divorce on American children, for example, finds statistically insignificant differences between children of divorced parents and children from intact families in various measures of well-being. Many studies of children of divorce fail to compare them to children from "intact" families, or fail to rule out predivorce conditions as causes. A ten-year longitudinal study released in Australia in June 1993 found that conflict between parents—whether divorced or not—is a frequent cause of emotional distress in children. This stress is mitigated, however, if the child has a close supportive relationship with at least one of the parents. Results also suggest that Australia's stronger welfare state and less adversarial divorce process may partly account for differences with U.S. findings.

Thus the evidence that divorce produces lasting damage to children is ambiguous at best, and I do not see how the ambiguities can be definitively resolved one way or the other. Complex and multiple social causation makes it naive to think we can conclusively test for a clear causal relationship between divorce and children's well-being. Without such certainty, however, it is wrong to suggest that the liberty of adults in their personal lives should be restricted. Galston and Etzioni endorse proposals that would impose a waiting period between the time a couple applied for divorce and the beginning of divorce proceedings. Divorce today already often drags on in prolonged acrimony. Children would likely benefit more from making it easier and less adversarial.

SINGLE PARENTHOOD AND CHILDREN

Although many Americans agree with me about divorce, they also agree with Quayle, Wilson, Galston, and others that single motherhood is undesirable for children, a deviant social condition that policy ought to try to correct. Etzioni claims that children of single parents receive less parental supervision and support than do children in two-parent families. It is certainly plausible that parenting is easier and more effective if two or more adults discuss the children's needs and provide different kinds of interactions for them. It does not follow, however, that the second adult must be a live-in husband. Some studies have found that the addition of any adult to a single-mother household, whether a relative, lover, or friend, tends to offset the tendency of single parents to relinquish decision making too early. Stephanie Coontz suggests that fine-tuned research on single-parent families would probably find that they are better for children in some respects and worse in others. For example, although adults in single-parent families spend less time supervising homework, single parents are less likely to pressure their children into social conformity and more likely to praise good grades.

Much less controversial is the claim that children in single-parent families are more often poor than those in two-parent families. One should be careful not to correlate poverty with single-parenthood, however; according to Coontz, a greater part of the increase in family poverty since 1979 has occurred in families with both spouses present, with only 38 percent concentrated in single-parent families. As many as 50 percent of single-parent families are likely to be poor, which is a shocking fact, but intact two-parent families are also increasingly likely to be poor, especially if the parents are in their twenties or younger.

DISCRIMINATION AGAINST SINGLE MOTHERS

It is harder to raise children alone than with at least one other adult, and the stresses of doing so can take their toll on children. I do not question that children in families that depend primarily on a woman's wage-earning ability are often disadvantaged. I do question the conclusion that getting single mothers married is the answer to childhood disadvantage.

Conservatives have always stated a preference for two-parent families. Having liberals join this chorus is disturbing because it makes such preference much more mainstream, thus legitimizing discrimination against single mothers. Single mothers commonly experience credit and employment discrimination. Discrimination against single mothers in renting apartments was legal until 1988, and continues to be routine in most cities. In a study of housing fairness in Pittsburgh in which I participated, most people questioned said that rental housing discrimination is normal in the area. Single mothers and their children also face biases in schools.

SINGLE MOTHERS AND POVERTY

The myth of a "culture of poverty" masks the reality of an economy of impoverishment. A lot of single mother families are broke, but they aren't broken.

In 1991, 47.1 percent of all female-headed families with children under 18 were below the official poverty line as were 19.6 percent of male-headed families with children and no wives present. The respective rates were 39.6 and 16.5 percent for whites, 60.5 and 31.7 percent for Blacks, and 60.1 and 29.4 percent for Latinos. In other words, single father families have very high rates of poverty, but single mother families have even higher rates.

It's not surprising that many single parent households are poor since the U.S. government neither assures affordable child care nor provides the universal child supports common in Western Europe. France, Britain, Denmark, and Sweden, for example, have similar or higher proportions of births to unmarried women without U.S. proportions of poverty.

Holly Sklar, Z Magazine, March 1993.

There is no hope that discrimination of this sort will ever end unless public discourse and government policy recognize that female-headed families are a viable, normal, and permanent family form, rather than something broken and deviant that policy should eradicate. Around one-third of families in the United States are headed by a woman alone; this proportion is about the same world-wide. The single-mother family is not going to fade away. Many women raise children alone because their husbands left them or because lack of access to contraception and abortion forced them to bear unwanted children. But many women are single mothers by choice. Women increasingly initiate divorces, and many single mothers report being happier after divorce and uninterested in remarriage, even when they are poorer.

SINGLE MOTHERHOOD CAN BE A CHOICE

Women who give birth out of wedlock, moreover, often have chosen to do so. Discussion of the "problem" of "illegitimate" births commonly assumes the image of the irresponsible and uneducated teenager (of color) as the unwed mother. When citing statistics about rising rates of out-of-wedlock birth, journalists and scholars rarely break them down by the mother's age, occupation, and so on. Although the majority of these births continue to be to young mothers, a rising proportion are to mid-life women with steady jobs who choose to have children. Women persist in such choices despite the fact that they are stigmatized and sometimes punished for them.

In a world where it can be argued that there are already too many people, it may sometimes be wrong for people to have babies. The planned birth of a third child in a stable two-parent family may be morally questionable from this point of view. But principles of equality and reproductive freedom must hold that there is nothing *more* wrong with a woman in her thirties with a stable job and income having a baby than with a similar married couple.

TEEN PARENTHOOD

If teen pregnancy is a social problem, this is not because the mothers are unmarried, but because they are young. They are inexperienced in the ways of the world and lack the skills necessary to get a job to support their children; once they become parents, their opportunities to develop those skills usually decrease. But these remain problems even when the women marry the young men with whom they have conceived children. Young inexperienced men today are just as ill prepared for parenting and just as unlikely to find decent jobs.

Although many young unmarried women who bear children do so because they are effectively denied access to abortions, many of these mothers want their babies. Today the prospects for meaningful work and a decent income appear dim to many youth, and especially to poor youth. Having a baby can give a young woman's life meaning, earn her respectful attention, make her feel grown up, and give her an excuse to exit the "wild" teenager scene that has begun to make her uncomfortable. Constructing an education and employment system that took girls as seriously as boys, that trained girls and boys for meaningful and available work would be a far more effective antidote to teen birth than reprimanding, stigmatizing, and punishing these girls.

Just as we should examine the assumption that something is wrong with a mid-life woman having a child without a husband, so we ought to ask a more radical question: just what in principle is more wrong in a young woman's bearing a child without a husband than in an older woman's doing so? When making their reproductive decisions, everyone ought to ask whether there are too many people in the world. Beyond that, I submit that we should affirm an unmarried young woman's right to bear a child as much as any other person's right.

REPRODUCTIVE CHOICES

There is reason to think that much of the world, including the United States, has plural childbearing cultures. Recently I heard a radio interview with an eighteen-year-old African-American woman in Washington, D.C. who had recently given birth to her second child. She affirmed wanting both children, and said that she planned to have no more. She lives in a subsidized apartment and participates in a job training program as a condition for receiving AFDC [Aid to Families with Dependent Children]. She resisted the interviewer's suggestion that there was something morally wrong or at least unfortunate with her choices and her life. She does not like being poor, and does not like having uncertain child care arrangements when she is away from her children. But she believes that in ten years, with hard work, social support, and good luck, she will have a community college degree and a decent job doing something she likes, as does her mother, now thirty-four.

There is nothing in principle wrong with such a pattern of having children first and getting education and job training later. Indeed, millions of white professional women currently in their fifties followed a similar pattern. Most of them, of course, were supported by husbands, and not state subsidy, when they stayed home to take care of their young children. Our racism, sexism, and classism are only thinly concealed when we praise stay-at-home mothers who are married, white, and middle class, and propose a limit of two years on welfare to unmarried, mostly nonwhite, and poor women who do the same thing. From a moral point of view, is there an important difference between the two kinds of dependence? If there is any serious commitment to equality in the United States, it must include an equal respect for people's reproductive choices.

"Children were meant to be nurtured by a man and woman together."

GAY-PARENTED FAMILIES ARE UNHEALTHY

Part I: Don Feder, Part II: George Grant and Mark A. Horne

In the following two-part viewpoint, Don Feder, George Grant, and Mark A. Horne argue that households headed by homosexuals are not healthy environments for children. In Part I, Feder, a syndicated columnist, contends that children raised by gay parents grow up witnessing an abnormal form of human sexuality and must deal with its long-term negative effects. In Part II, Grant and Horne maintain that the children of homosexuals live in unstable environments where they are likely to be harmed by exposure to explicit sexuality. Grant and Horne are the authors of *Legislating Immorality: The Homosexual Movement Comes Out of the Closet*, from which Part II of this viewpoint is excerpted.

As you read, consider the following questions:

1. According to Feder, what did Dr. Paul Cameron discover in his study of research on children living in households with at least one homosexual?
2. According to Maggie Gallagher, as quoted by Grant and Horne, in what way have states made marriage a "legal fiction"?
3. According to Grant and Horne, what were the motives of the homosexual activists who attempted to pass a domestic-partnership ordinance in San Francisco?

Part I: Don Feder, "Kids Raised by Homosexuals Traumatized," *Human Events*, October 16, 1993. Reprinted by permission of Don Feder and Creators Syndicate. Part II: Taken from *Legislating Immorality* by George Grant and Mark A. Horne. Copyright 1993, Mariposa Ltd. Used by permission of the publisher, Moody Press.

I

Regarding his colleagues' support for gay adoption/custody, psychologist Joe Nicolosi observes: "One of the beautiful things about a democracy is that social scientists can ruin a generation, and then come back 20 years later with our objective measures to validate what common sense should have told us."

Social science is far from the only transgressor here. Recently, a juvenile court commissioner in Whatcom County, Washington, ordered a three-year-old boy placed with two male homosexuals as the first step toward adoption.

The child is the center of a raging controversy. His mother, who had placed him for adoption, changed her mind when she learned of the arrangement. "I don't want my son raised like that," says Megan Lucas. But that is precisely the way her son will be raised, if Washington State has its way. [In 1994, the state of Washington allowed the adoption.]

In this matter, courts are anything but consistent. In September 1993, a Virginia judge took a child away from his mother and her lesbian lover, awarding custody to the maternal grandmother.

In a few states, when homosexuality is an aspect of divorce, courts invariably grant custody to the heterosexual parent. In others, it's a factor but by no means decisive. New York, New Jersey, Vermont, Minnesota and California allow gay adoption, usually by the partner of a biological parent.

Psychologists have added their voices to the trendy chorus. The American Psychological Association complains that courts "often have assumed that . . . children are likely to be emotionally harmed, subject to molestation, impaired in gender role development or themselves homosexual. None of these assumptions is supported by extant research data."

But there was a time when psychologists insisted there were no long-term effects of divorce on children. Then researchers like Judith Wallerstein discovered that the children of divorce are far more likely to be withdrawn and afraid of commitment.

BIASED CLAIMS
In the early 1970s, Jay Belsky, a Pennsylvania State University psychologist, was running around telling anyone who would listen that there was nothing wrong with putting infants in day care. Today, he's one of the most outspoken critics of collective child-rearing, contending that children placed in day care at an early age form weak parental attachments and have emotional

problems later in life.

When it comes to child welfare, the claims of social scientists must be viewed with extreme skepticism.

Most researchers, who are biased in favor of homosexuals, ignore their own data. Dr. Paul Cameron, Ph.D., of the Family Research Institute has surveyed the admittedly scant findings of his profession on children raised in households with at least one homosexual.

Developing Healthy Sexual Identities

Regardless of what courts rule, children need a same-sex and an opposite-sex parent to have the best chance to develop healthy sexual identities. Those in single-parent households already are disadvantaged because one of the sexes is missing. Some single parents understand this "gender deficit" and work mightily to ensure that their children receive guidance from grandparents or other role models who represent the sexes evenly. In a homosexual household, the problem is compounded by the embrace of same-sex sexuality within the home itself. Children, who in an androgynous culture are having an increasingly hard time trying to establish basic, confident gender identities, cannot possibly be helped by seeing "mom" kiss "mom" or "dad" kiss "dad."

Robert H. Knight, *Insight*, July 25, 1994.

In these studies, between 8% and 33% of adult respondents said they considered themselves homosexual or bisexual, far above the national norm of 2% of the adult male population.

How surprising is this? In almost every area, parental behavior has a profound, at times predominant, impact on children. The children of smokers frequently become smokers. Kids from abusive homes often become abusers. Children from broken homes are more likely to divorce. Only in the case of homosexuality are we asked to believe that what happens in the home is irrelevant to emotional development.

Children Need Heterosexual Parents

Jaki Edwards of Milpitas, Calif., who runs a support and recovery program for those coming out of the homosexual lifestyle and their families, has knowledge beyond questionnaires and graphs. From age 10 to 16, she and a younger brother lived with their lesbian mother and a succession of her companions.

"I realize that homosexuals feel they can give a child love and support that even many straight families can't provide," Edwards admits, "but I've been there. I know the finger-pointing and the shame one carries.

"For years, you struggle with the thought that you might be a homosexual. People say 'like mother, like daughter.' Most of us become promiscuous to prove we're straight."

The absence of role models presents its own problems. "How will a man raised by two men know how to relate to a woman? A woman brought up like this doesn't know how to emotionally connect with men. I had to struggle for years to believe a man could really love me."

How many lives will be broken, how many little experiments will suffer in silence (unobserved by omniscient researchers) before courts and social scientists learn you can't fool nature? Children were meant to be nurtured by a man and woman together. Absent that, at least they shouldn't be placed in a situation where a distorted version of human sexuality is presented as the norm, to satisfy the latest bizarre demands for equality.

II

One part of the homosexual agenda is to legally recognize homosexual "marriages" and allow them to "have" children—that is, to adopt them. For the government to recognize heterosexual marriages while refusing to recognize homosexual "marriages," they claim, is a blatant case of inequality before the law.

MARRIAGE IS A LEGAL FICTION

Interestingly, the homosexual case is bolstered by the fact that, in many situations, the government *does not* recognize heterosexual marriages. As Maggie Gallagher points out, by permitting no-fault divorce, states have made marriage a veritable legal fiction. She uses a couple, Jim and Mary—who are in the throes of divorce proceedings—to demonstrate her assertion:

> When Mary agreed to live in the same house with Jim and accept his financial support and offer her own paid and unpaid labor to the household, to sleep in the same bed and bear his children, she did so because she thought she was married. Had Jim asked her to do these things for him without getting married, she would have slapped his face. Mary knew what marriage meant. The example of her parents and the teachings of her religion gave her a concrete idea of the unwritten law. It meant the two became one flesh, one family. It was a lifetime commitment. But the state of California informed her that she was not allowed to make or to accept lifetime commitments. No-fault divorce gave judges, at the request of one half a couple, the right to de-

cide when a marriage had irretrievably broken down. They decided by and large that wanderlust would be a state-protected emotion, while loyalty was on its own. In a cruel display of raw judicial power, the state of California made Mary a single woman again, without protecting her interests and without requiring her consent.

With the advent of no-fault divorce laws, the state no longer obligates couples to fulfill the contractual agreement they made with each other when they got married. As far as the government is concerned, men must have more respect for their credit cards than for their wives.

Yet even with marriage in such a state of disrepair, homosexuals still find it too restrictive. In 1989, for example, homosexual advocates attempted to pass a "domestic partnership" ordinance in San Francisco. This law was to ensure that the city and county governments would not "discriminate against domestic partners" or use "marital status as a factor in any decision, policy, or practice unless it uses domestic partnership as a factor in the same way." The upshot of the bill was that live-in lovers of government employees could get the same benefits as spouses.

DOMESTIC PARTNERSHIP IS NOT MARRIAGE

The problem with the ordinance is simply that "domestic partners" are not the same as married couples. This becomes evident when one looks at how these partnerships can be ended: "A domestic partnership ends when . . . one partner sends the other a written notice that he or she has ended the partnership." The only requirement is that the notice be notarized and turned in to the bureaucracy.

Just as the things homosexuals do are not simply the same-sex equivalent of what heterosexuals do, homosexual "marriage" is not the same-sex equivalent of heterosexual marriage. Although it is good propaganda for homosexuals to claim that "homophobic" marriage laws discourage them from having "stable relationships," there is no convincing evidence that they even want stable relationships. The only thing we do know is that they want spousal benefits for whoever happens to be living with someone.

FAMILY VALUES?

And when it comes to children, the "family values" of homosexuals become even more disturbing. It is by no means sensationalistic to weigh the impact of the homosexual lifestyle on the emotional health of children in homosexual "families."

Out magazine, for instance, published an article in 1993 containing advice for "queer moms" who need to "get out of the house and into somebody's pants." The writer, Susie Bright, whose latest book is *Susie Bright's Sexual Reality: A Virtual Sex World Reader*, mentions that it is extremely important to have lots of baby-sitters because "we are more often than not relying on an extended family of 'aunts,' 'godmothers,' and friends who are often the very people we'd like to spend an evening with."

The need for baby-sitters raises a problem, however:

> But teenage baby-sitters are often squeamish about sex, not to mention homosexuality. Who knows what sort of parents they have, and how much they confide in them? The grim side of a gay mom's social life is that underneath her swinging-single exterior, she is always worried that someone will try to take her kid away. The law is not on our side. No matter what contracts we've signed with donors, friendly fathers, or sperm banks, the whole area of child custody and gay parenting is up for grabs.

This sounds horrible, of course. Yet when the author of the article tells a prospective baby-sitter what she must be willing to put up with, we get a rare glimpse at the world that children of homosexuals are raised to take for granted:

> I take the out-of-the-closet or out-of-my-house approach. I told my first teenage baby-sitter that I was queer, that I wrote about sex for a living, and that my house was full of erotic art. I said, "If your parents would disapprove of you working here, or if it's not your cup of tea, then this baby-sitting job is not for you."

So the cat's out of the bag. Bright considers it repressive that some people think it is wrong and should be illegal to raise children in the presence of pornography. What wonderful "family values."

| "Families headed by lesbians and gays are working out successfully."

GAY-PARENTED FAMILIES ARE HEALTHY

April Martin

April Martin, a psychologist, is the author of *The Lesbian and Gay Parenting Book: Creating and Raising Our Families*. In the following viewpoint, Martin contends that families headed by gays and lesbians are no less stable than families headed by heterosexual parents. According to Martin, no studies have shown that a parent's homosexuality affects a child's emotional health, sexual orientation, or social adjustment. Society should therefore respect and support the rights of lesbians and gays who wish to become parents, she concludes.

As you read, consider the following questions:

1. Which two groups oppose lesbian- and gay-headed families, according to Martin?
2. For what reasons do gays and lesbians choose to become parents, in Martin's opinion?
3. In the author's opinion, why are gays and lesbians more willing to adopt hard-to-place children?

Lesbian and gay parents are not a new phenomenon. There are an estimated 5 million to 6 million of them in this country, most of whom became parents in the context of a heterosexual marriage before they were fully aware of their sexual orientation. What is new, however, is that since the 1970s lesbians and gay men, perhaps tens of thousands, are choosing to become parents through adoption and artificial insemination. As the stigma evaporates and visibility increases, word is getting around among adoption, health care and child welfare professionals that families headed by lesbians and gays are working out successfully.

My own daughter will be 13 soon, and our son is almost 10. My life partner, a woman, and I began to plan this family 16 years ago. As we struggle to fit soccer practice, orthodontia appointments, music lessons, homework and family time into our schedules, we find it bewildering that anyone sees us as a threat to their values. We visit the grandparents, go to PTA meetings, attend church and have the occasional shopping spree. We hold strong ideas about what is important: education, ethics, responsibility, good manners—not exactly revolutionary fare.

SOCIAL PREJUDICE

Still, we live our lives against a backdrop of social prejudice. Antigay initiatives that threaten to create danger and suffering for our families are being proposed in many states. One proposal in Washington state would take children away from their lesbian or gay parents and place them in foster care—an astonishing cruelty in the name of family values.

Opposition to lesbian and gay families seems to come from two very different voices: the extremists of the Christian right, and a larger group of serious-minded people who aren't familiar with gay-parented families. There's not much we can say to the Christian far right, because they don't seem to be listening. They construct science-fiction horror stories to portray us as sexual abusers and "recruiters" of children. They cite bogus "research studies"—not compiled by reputable universities but by their own political organizations—to show that children with lesbian moms will grow up to be homosexual. They warn that gay parents will transmit AIDS to children, despite facts showing that children's HIV infections typically are acquired in the wombs of heterosexual mothers. They also ignore the fact that lesbians are in the lowest HIV group of the population and that gay men who are dealing with HIV generally are not the people seeking to become parents. They point to numerous studies showing that children of single mothers fare less well, ignoring the fact that lesbians in stable life-partnerships are not "single" in any but the strict legal sense and thus do not suffer the economic disadvantages which account for the plight of many single-parent families.

The Christian far right opposes school curricula that teach tolerance for diverse families, warning that children might get the idea that homosexuality is acceptable. They seem to assume that if heterosexual children were to see homosexuality as okay, nothing would stop them from rushing out and changing their sexual orientations. The vigorous crusaders dedicated to fighting lesbian- and gay-parented families clearly have more than reason invested in their position, and it is unlikely to be modified by exposure to the reality of who we are.

ENTITLED TO RAISE CHILDREN

More and more gay fathers are deciding to come out, according to Howard Levin, president of Gay Fathers of New York, who says he saw a doubling in membership in his group between 1991 and 1993. It's part of what gay fathers like Levin see as new awareness in the gay movement: that gays and lesbians are not only capable, but entitled to raise children.

Along with the new visibility of gay fathers, another historic event is taking place: openly gay and lesbian parents deciding to become parents through a variety of inventive, and even biological, means. Some experts, such as Charlotte Patterson, a University of Virginia psychologist, are proclaiming it "a gay baby boom."

To Patterson's mind, gay people, who have lived their adult lives within the gay community, are choosing adoption, alternative insemination (the politically correct synonym for "artificial" insemination) and surrogate motherhood as a way of having a family life without compromising hard-won gay and lesbian identities. Seen together, these two movements—closeted gay parents coming out and openly gay people becoming parents—are constituting nothing less than a rethinking of "family values," challenging both the gay community's and the far-right's sense of itself.

Doug Sadownick, *Genre*, June/July 1993.

We very much want a dialogue, however, with those who bring unfamiliarity, rather than bigotry, to the issue. Their doubts about whether we can truly provide for the needs of children are precisely our concerns as well. We lesbians and gay men choose to become parents for the same reasons heterosexuals do: to impart our love, our knowledge and our heritages to our children and to experience the joy of helping a young heart and mind develop. Ultimately, we desire to fulfill some of what is best in humanity.

Not one of us would bring a child into our homes if we hadn't explored some hard questions: Can children grow up healthy with gay parents? What are their needs for role models of their own or the opposite gender? Are they likely to be harmed by prejudice? Will they have difficulties with friends or social life? Will they be confused about their own sexuality? These issues are vitally important to us.

STUDY RESULTS

Furthermore, judges, legislatures, educators and health care professionals also are asking the same questions. Gradually, they are familiarizing themselves with the research compiled during the last 15 years or so. What we know is based on approximately two dozen studies conducted by psychologists, psychiatrists and social workers. Most of the studies have compared the development of children raised by lesbian mothers or, in some cases, children raised by gay fathers with the development of children raised by heterosexual parents. According to Dr. Charlotte Patterson of the University of Virginia, writing in a 1992 issue of *Child Development* (considered the best journal in the field), a review of this research reveals that:

• Not a single study showed any difference in the children's level of emotional adjustment, whether raised by heterosexual or gay parents.

• Children raised by lesbian or gay parents were no more or less likely to be homosexual than other children.

• Boys showed no differences in tendency toward "masculine" behavior, mannerisms or interests, and girls showed no differences in "femininity."

• Despite the existence of social prejudice, children with lesbian or gay parents did just as well as other children socially and academically.

If myths about lesbians and gay men were true of us, I would agree that we shouldn't raise children. We are a highly diverse group, and though the media is fond of focusing on drag queens and motorcycle dykes, most of us less colorful folks have been invisible. This gradually is changing as more and more of us come out, giving our parents, extended families, neighbors and coworkers a chance to see us as real human beings.

THE REALITIES OF GAY PARENTHOOD

Here are some of the realities:

Lesbians and gay men don't become parents accidentally. No one pressures them into parenthood. The ones who choose it are those with domestic enthusiasm and nurturing temperaments. Prospective parents often spend months and years in "considering parenthood" workshops to explore whether they realistically have the emotional, physical, financial, spiritual and community resources to be good parents. They discuss it with family, friends, clergy and psychotherapists. The children we adopt or conceive are among the most wanted and prepared for children on earth. Someday, perhaps, this standard will become the standard for all parents—even those who can create families without having to think about it.

Contrary to the Christian far right's portrayal of lesbians and gay men as sex-obsessed and depraved, our families are no more about sex than anyone else's. On an exhausting morning after I've stayed up late typing my daughter's science report, when there are school lunches to be packed and disputes to be settled about whose turn it is to play Nintendo, I could fall over laughing at the thought. We are an affectionate family—lots of hugging and kissing—but like most families, we believe that sexual activity is an extremely private matter. We respect our children's modesty and expect them to respect ours.

Lesbians do not hate men. Gay men do not hate women. We go out of our way to ensure that there are role models of the other gender in our children's lives. Along with other lesbian mothers, I am aware that my son needs someone with whom he can talk about "guy" things, and I want my children to grow up knowing and appreciating men. My kids have an adoring grandfather, and we have cultivated the children's relationships with some trusted male friends. (Unfortunately, many lesbians who conceive through artificial insemination are forced to use anonymous sperm donors, because laws fail to protect them from potentially devastating custody battles. If they had the same protection as families formed by adoption, they would be freer to use sperm donors whose identities are known to them and could more easily include biological fathers in their children's lives.)

Lesbian and gay parents are prepared to accept their children's sexuality—whatever it may be. We assume that 90 to 95 percent of them will be heterosexual. We know from our own experience of being raised by heterosexual parents, in a heterosexual society, that sexual orientation is not subject to external dictates. We raise our children to be themselves.

And here's the part that surprised even many of us: It appears similarly impossible to influence gender-role behavior. I know some feminist lesbians who intended to raise daughters who could fix a car and wouldn't worry about hairdo and makeup. Lo and behold, they tell me, laughing, the universe sent them girls who want nail polish and Barbie dolls. They lovingly cave in, just as I have with a son who is wild for the goony machismo of the World Wrestling Federation. Values and character are things we can influence; preferences are to be discovered and accepted.

What makes our families different is not the nature of our parenting efforts, but the constellations of the families. The *Leave It to Beaver* model—one parent of each gender, both biologically related to the child, he the breadwinner, she the cookie baker—often is proffered as a societal standard, with worries that deviations may adversely affect children. In truth, this child-rearing arrangement is not the norm in many cultures and has never been as widespread in ours as the nostalgists would have us believe. Our experience, supported by child-development research and echoed by our kids themselves, shows that it is love—not biology—that makes a family. Our children have no trouble accepting what is common in many other societies—namely, that people who create you may not necessarily be the parents who raise you. Though they are given full and truthful information about their origins, their bonds are with those who are there to soothe a tummy ache, discuss a school problem or show them the wonders of a firefly.

But what about dealing with the larger world? Is it unfair to raise a child who may experience antigay bias because of his or her parents? Well, yes. It's as unfair as raising a female child in a sexist world or a child of color in a racist society. Prejudice is a tragic fact and one that I expect our children will make a contribution toward fighting when they grow up. Like other families who experience oppression, we try to give our children the tools to deal with it: self-esteem, social consciousness and courage.

In reality, however, the actual oppression they experience is far less than any of us would have imagined. My children have never been teased or harassed. They are popular and well-liked. The welcome we have found from our schools, neighborhood and friends has been heartwarming. I'm sure that if parents of their classmates had been polled before they knew us, many would have flatly disapproved of a two-mom family. Yet today their kids and ours share sleep-over dates, and we rely on each other for babysitting and mutual support. What's more, I've heard stories such as this from families all over the country, not just in liberal, urban areas. It sustains my faith that people will discard negative stereotypes that conflict with their face-to-face experience.

THE ISSUES AT STAKE

The issues at stake here are only partly about the rights of lesbians and gay men to parent and only partly about the legal and social rights of children in a variety of family structures. Also at stake are the rights of some children to have homes at all. Lesbians and gay men, who know the experience of being thrown away by society, frequently are willing to adopt children who are significantly physically and emotionally disabled. To deny lesbians and gay men the right to adopt, as do the states of New Hampshire and Florida and as many state legislatures are considering doing, is cruel and pointless. It condemns these children to institutional and foster care, at taxpayer expense, for no humane reason.

I share with families of any constellation a concern about the violence in our society; the failures of our educational systems; and the large numbers of young people damaged by drugs, alcohol, teenage pregnancy and lack of hope. It is my wish that we can work together to find solutions. As do many lesbian and gay parents, I teach my children tolerance for goodwilled people whose customs, characteristics or beliefs differ from mine. It is hard to see how teaching tolerance for our families and granting them basic legal protections does any harm to those who live differently—even to the unfortunate minority who teach their children to fear and hate.

PERIODICAL BIBLIOGRAPHY

The following articles have been selected to supplement the diverse views presented in this chapter. Addresses are provided for periodicals not indexed in the *Readers' Guide to Periodical Literature*, the *Alternative Press Index*, the *Social Sciences Index*, or the *Index to Legal Periodicals and Books*.

Charles Augustus Ballard	"Prodigal Dad: How We Bring Fathers Home to Their Children," *Policy Review*, Winter 1995.
Fred A. Bernstein	"This Child Does Have Two Mothers . . . and a Sperm Donor with Visitation," *New York University Review of Law & Social Change*, 1996.
Peggy Ellsberg	"What's Wrong with Family Values?" *America*, April 3, 1993.
Jean Bethke Elshtain	"Family Matters: The Plight of America's Children," *Christian Century*, July 14–21, 1993.
Steven Flanders	"The Benefits of Marriage," *Public Interest*, Summer 1996.
Michele Ingrassia	"Endangered Family," *Newsweek*, August 30, 1993.
Janine Jackson	"The 'Crisis' of Teen Pregnancy: Girls Pay the Price for Media Distortion," *Extra!*, March/April 1994.
Barbara Kantrowitz	"Gay Families Come Out," *Newsweek*, November 4, 1996.
Linda S. Lichter	"Home Truths," *Commentary*, June 1994.
Mike Males	"In Defense of Teenage Mothers," *Progressive*, August 1994.
David Popenoe	"A World Without Fathers," *Wilson Quarterly*, Spring 1996.
Linda B. Rubin	"People Don't Know Right from Wrong Anymore," *Tikkun*, January/February 1994.
Holly Sklar	"The Upperclass and Mothers N the Hood," *Z Magazine*, March 1993.
Judith Stacey	"Dan Quayle's Revenge: The New Family Values Crusade," *Nation*, July 25–August 1, 1994.
William Tucker	"All in the Family," *National Review*, March 6, 1995.

CHAPTER 2

HOW HAVE DIVORCE LAW REFORMS AFFECTED THE FAMILY?

CHAPTER PREFACE

California passed the first no-fault divorce laws in the country in 1969, and all fifty states had instituted some form of no-fault divorce by 1985. Before no-fault, couples seeking to divorce were required to prove in court that one spouse had committed a wrongdoing. Under no-fault laws, no such grounds are required, and divorce is much easier to obtain. Proponents of reform intended the new divorce laws to accomplish two goals: end the practice of fabricating fault, which had led couples to lie in court; and provide a less acrimonious way for couples with children to divorce.

However, lawmakers in many states have begun to advocate reforming divorce laws again. These lawmakers, joined by many religious leaders and policymakers, contend that by making divorce easy, no-fault divorce laws have rendered the marriage contract meaningless and have undermined the family's value to society. One result of the no-fault laws, the critics argue, has been an increase in the number of divorces—many of them in families with children. It is the children, they assert, that divorce affects most directly and most severely. According to David Blankenhorn, president of the Institute for American Values in New York, "The children of divorce have not been served by this process. They've been damaged. The evidence is overwhelming that this has maimed an entire generation of children."

Many experts challenge the assumptions that underlie these efforts to change the laws. They maintain that the original reasons that divorce laws were changed are still valid. Michael Robbins, the former chair of the Michigan bar's family law section, contends that "the reason no-fault swept across the country was a recognition on the part of individuals and legislators that no law had the power to force people to stay together when they didn't want to. Before 1969, under the fault system people were saying and doing almost anything to get around the law." These experts also question the argument that children of divorced parents develop behavioral problems later in life. For example, sociologist Andrew Cherlin argues, "When we look at young adults whose parents divorce, there's no question that they're at higher risk of mental health problems and other difficulties. Even so, most of them don't actually show those difficulties. So while it's a mistake to say that divorce doesn't hurt kids, the data also contradict the belief that divorce is inevitably a disaster for most children."

The effects of divorce on children have many implications for society. The viewpoints in the following chapter debate whether reforming divorce laws can ameliorate such potential harms.

| "Today, while it still takes two to marry, it takes only one to divorce."

NO-FAULT DIVORCE LAWS HAVE HARMED THE FAMILY

Maggie Gallagher

Maggie Gallagher is the author of *Enemies of Eros* and *The Abolition of Marriage: How We Destroy Lasting Love*, from which the following viewpoint is excerpted. Gallagher contends that when states began to change their divorce laws from a fault-based to a no-fault system, the institutions of marriage and family were effectively undermined. The steadily rising divorce rates that resulted from these legal changes, she argues, have contributed to various problems—especially for women and children. She concludes, therefore, that divorce laws must be reformed in order to make divorce more difficult to obtain.

As you read, consider the following questions:

1. What does the phrase "unilateral divorce" mean, according to the author?
2. In Gallagher's opinion, what were the reasons for instituting the first no-fault divorce laws?
3. What changes to divorce laws does Gallagher advocate?

In 1970 Mary, a nice Catholic twenty-something California girl, tried to commit an illegal act.

She and her boyfriend Jim decided to wed: They had blood tests and got a license; they engaged a priest to preside at the ceremony. The bride donned a white satin gown, the groom a tuxedo, and they exchanged vows. Afterward, she took his name. To all outward appearances, Mary and Jim were married. Everyone said so.

MARRIAGE OUTLAWED

But 1970 was the year the state of California created no-fault divorce. With that act, and with no fanfare and little public debate, California quietly outlawed marriage.

Mary did not find this out until nearly a decade later when her husband flew off to Los Angeles on a business trip, never to return. Mary received a letter in which Jim explained he had married too young and needed to "find himself." She was left with two kids, $12,000 from the sale of the house, and $300 a month in child support.

When Mary agreed to live with Jim, to accept his financial support and offer her own labor (paid and unpaid) to the household and to sleep in the same bed and bear his children, she did so because she thought she was married. Had Jim asked her to do these things for him without marriage, she would have undoubtedly slapped his face. Mary knew what marriage meant. The example of her parents and the teaching of her religion made the unspoken concrete: Marriage meant two individuals became one flesh, one family. It was a lifetime commitment.

But the state of California later informed her that she was not allowed to make or accept lifetime commitments. No-fault divorce gave judges, at the request of one-half of the couple, the right to decide when a marriage had irretrievably broken down. The state decided that, by and large, wanderlust would be protected by law, while loyalty was on its own. In a cruel display of raw judicial power, the state of California made Mary a single woman again, without protecting her interest and without her consent.

What happened to Mary in California in 1970 happened to many other people in many other parts of the country as state after state feverishly jumped on the no-fault bandwagon. By the early eighties, the revolution was complete: Eighteen states had eliminated fault grounds for divorce altogether; almost all the rest offered a no-fault divorce option. Unlike many European countries, which attach waiting periods as long as five to seven years before a man or woman may obtain a no-fault divorce against an unconsenting spouse, American legislatures opted for quick and easy spouse disposal. Why wait to bury a dead marriage, they reasoned? Most states require less than a year's separation for a no-fault divorce.

UNILATERAL DIVORCE

No-fault legislation was supposed to permit a couple to get a divorce by mutual consent. No longer, reformers promised, would a perfectly amicable divorcing couple have to pretend the husband was a cruel philanderer to get the courts to give them a divorce. But what no-fault laws actually did was something dramatically different: Under the guise of making a merely technical adjustment to the legal mechanics of divorce, the legal profession radically transformed the legal and moral basis of marriage. It created a new beast: not no-fault, but unilateral divorce. Today, while it still takes two to marry, it takes only one to divorce.

Divorce by mutual-consent divorce is rare. Over 80 percent of divorces are now the unilateral choice of one partner. Americans were given the freedom to sever the marriage tie at any time and for any reason and so lost the ability to make a permanent, binding commitment. We gained the right to divorce and in the process lost the right to marry.

And this is the remarkable thing: No one noticed.

Rings and vows were exchanged, garters thrown, cakes cut, households set up, and children born. People continued to use the same word—marriage—to describe this radically new social institution that had been created, a relation that, legally speaking, more closely resembles taking a concubine than giving oneself to a spouse.

Divorce reformers imagined that they could ease the passage of disgruntled individuals out of bad marriages and yet retain intact the institution of marriage. No-fault divorce, they said (and we believed) is only a humane way of disposing of dead marriages. It doesn't affect the vitality of the truly wed.

This reform is often portrayed as an increase in individual choice or freedom. But the legal changes that constitute the divorce revolution can more accurately be described as *a shift in power*: from the married to the unmarried in general, from the spouse who wants to stay married to the spouse who wants to leave, from the person who wants to commit to the person who wants the right to revoke his or her commitments.

The reformers did not calculate what would happen once the message contained in the new marriage laws sank in. They never pondered what it would be like to get married and yet know that one's spouse not only could leave at any time, but also had an absolute right to do so. They never contemplated the anxiety that burdened young men and women who consider betting their futures in a game heavily weighted in favor of the unfaithful, the immature, the betrayer.

A FAILED REVOLUTION

The divorce revolution has been a failure, and the majority of Americans know it. The national debate is shifting from divorce to marriage and the need to rebuild a family culture based on enduring marital relationships. Now, Michigan and several other states are at the forefront of a pro-family counterrevolution. Let us hope that the era of no-fault divorce is headed for the trash-heap of history.

Gleaves Whitney, Crisis, May 1996.

The spouse who decides to divorce has a liberating sense of mastery, one of the key components of personal happiness. He or she is leaving, breaking free, reaching for the exhilarating headlong embrace of change, which, with its psychic echoes of the original adolescent break from family, can boost self-esteem.

But being divorced reinforces exactly the opposite sense of life. Being divorced does not feel like an act of personal courage, for the simple reason that it is not an act at all. It is something that happens to a spouse and over which, thanks to no-fault legislation, the spouse has no say at all. The spouse who leaves learns that love dies. The spouse who is left learns that love betrays, that he or she has no control over the terms of marriage. Neither the culture nor the courts will enforce any commitment. The only rule is, He who wants out, wins. . . .

THE MURDER OF MARRIAGE

The murder of marriage is a particular atrocity because it was mostly the act of a small and narrow elite. As difficult as it is to believe, the historical record is fairly clear: In the early seventies marriage was radically transformed and the traditional marriage commitment outlawed in a way that has endangered the economic and emotional well-being of millions of women and children, largely to please lawyers.

In 1966, before the no-fault revolution, only 13 percent of Americans believed divorce laws were too strict. As Harvard professor of law Mary Ann Glendon notes, "Discontent with fault-based divorce seems to have been felt more acutely by mental-health professionals and academics than by the citizenry in general." It was not an anguished public, chained by marriage vows, that demanded divorce as a right. The revolution was made by the determined whine of lawyers, judges, psychiatrists, marriage counselors, academics, and goo-goo-eyed reformers who objected to, of all things, the amount of hypocrisy contained in the law.

Fault-based divorce, they believed, forced couples who wanted to split to fabricate evidence of adultery or mental cruelty in order to get a divorce. Lawyers were forced to manufacture, and judges were forced to pretend to believe, fabricated evidence, thus undermining the public's respect for the legal profession.

Has no-fault been a success? If you ask divorce lawyers, judges, and legal scholars, they'll say, Yes, certainly. And if the purpose of our legal system is to create better working conditions for lawyers, then they are right. Every survey of family court judges and divorce lawyers reveals that the legal profession remains immensely satisfied, that the no-fault divorce revolution has achieved its goals: eliminating "hypocrisy," raising the social status of divorce lawyers, and reducing acrimony around divorce—or at least the amount of acrimony to which judges and lawyers are exposed. An Iowa evaluation concluded, for example, that according to "the satisfied majority both of judges and attorneys" no-fault divorces resulted in "a more honest and civilized approach void of . . . fraud, perjury and abuse." A poll of Nebraska judges found that two-thirds agreed no-fault laws had lessened animosity between divorcing parties. These judges also acknowledged the laws had introduced unilateral divorce, but they seemed unconcerned by the fact.

No-Fault Divorce and Divorce Rates

The chorus of approval for no-fault divorces was amplified by initial studies that nearly unanimously concluded that these changes in the law had little effect on the divorce rate. For ten years these studies, which confirmed what the intelligentsia wanted to hear, remained the unchallenged conventional wisdom: The law, we were told, was utterly impotent to influence people's behavior. You can't legislate morality.

But evaluating the effect of the law on divorce rates turned out to be tricky. Not only do state statutes vary, but different states changed different aspects of divorce law. Some states merely added no-fault to other grounds for divorce. Others abolished fault altogether. Still others cut waiting periods.

Many of the earlier studies assumed that all the changes lumped under the no-fault rubric had the same effect on divorce rates. Moreover, in many cases, states officially passed "no-fault" laws only after judges had already effectively changed legal practices to ease divorce. This made it difficult to assess the effect on divorce rates of statutory changes that largely codified what judges were already doing. To add to the confusion, many other states were suddenly labeled no-fault states, not because the law had changed, but because they were included in a catalog of no-fault jurisdictions assembled for a 1974 listing in an influential journal, Family Law Quarterly. Since many early researchers relied on this listing as definitive evidence of when states adopted no-fault divorce (when in fact the law had not changed or had changed much earlier), it called into question their conclusion that changes in the law had no effect.

Two recent studies, however, using different methods of analysis independently concluded that some of the changes in divorce law did increase the divorce rate in at least some jurisdictions—and by as much as 20 percent and 25 percent. At least one researcher found that no-fault divorce increased the divorce rate among certain families with children, in particular. . . .

THE DISAPPEARANCE OF MARRIAGE

Marriage will not by some mystical process revive, and it may not even survive. The tragic experience of the African American family should warn us that it is indeed possible for marriage, as a durable child-rearing bond, to virtually disappear. The forces undermining the married family in modern society are many and deep: the decline in male wages, the deteriorating neighborhoods and schools, the graying of America and the consequent diversion of resources from children to the elderly, and the sexual revolution.

Above all, a 50 percent to 60 percent divorce rate—tolerated for a generation—in itself sets in motion a dynamic of decline that will not spontaneously reverse itself. In a divorce culture, anxious married couples sharply limit their investment in each other and in children. As the marriage contract becomes attenuated and unenforceable, fewer married women feel safe bearing children. And as fewer single women see any need to marry to have children, the illegitimacy rate soars. Meanwhile, their children—the children of divorce—are themselves at higher risk of divorce and unwed parenthood, a phenomenon that by itself fuels a dangerously downward spiral of marital decay.

To break the cycle requires first and foremost strengthening the law of marriage. The first step is to end unilateral divorce. Making divorce quick and easy at the discretion of one partner has led to a surge in the divorce rate everywhere it has been tried, for reasons obvious to anyone who has ever been married. Recent research suggests such changes in divorce law may account for as much as 25 percent of the increase in the divorce rate.

Reforming no-fault divorce is more than a tactical necessity. Simple decency requires that the law retreat from relentlessly favoring the spouse who leaves in no-fault divorces and place some minimal power back into the hands of the spouse who is being left. Imposing a five- to seven-year waiting period for contested no-fault divorces (as do many European jurisdictions) would serve the ends of both justice and prudence: raising the number of marriages that ultimately succeed, while at the very least ensuring that those who want a quick and easy divorce will have to negotiate with their marriage partner in order to get it.

A Legal Contract

Stabilizing marriage law also requires finding new mechanisms for making sure the marriage contract has legal force. One reason for America's seemingly relentless drift toward more and more lenient divorce laws is federalism: since states are required to recognize each others' divorces, divorce law has tended to be driven by the most permissive state. A New York husband who wants to divorce his wife can, after a quick trip to Reno, come back a free man, regardless of New York law. One solution is to make the marriage contract explicit, rather than implicit: give married couples a copy of the marriage contract now drawn up for them by state legislatures. Federal law should require that state courts recognize the validity of marriage contracts of other states, and should require the use of the written contract as the basis for divorce.

Finally, some legal avenue should also be opened for those who wish, in marrying, to make an enduring commitment. At the very least the law should support permanent marriage by giving people the option of making one. Prenuptial agreements are routinely used to protect the wealthier spouse in the event of a divorce. If the law can limit marital liability, should it not, at the very least, accommodate those who—out of love, longing, religion, or ideals—seek to extend it? A prenuptial covenant, permitting divorce only for serious cause, or even, if the couple wished, prohibiting it altogether, should be a legally enforceable option.

"The only thing squelching no-fault will do is to recreate the sham of another era, when couples who wanted to divorce were obliged to invent affairs and abuse."

THE HARMS OF NO-FAULT DIVORCE LAWS HAVE BEEN EXAGGERATED

Hanna Rosin

In the following viewpoint, Hanna Rosin challenges the assumption made by many commentators that no-fault divorce laws have harmed families and society. She maintains that divorce rates have been rising steadily since the middle of the nineteenth century; no-fault divorce has merely contributed to this established trend, she insists. Although Rosin agrees that current divorce laws could be made more equitable, she opposes returning to a fault-based system. Rosin is an associate editor at the *New Republic*, a journal of social and political commentary.

As you read, consider the following questions:

1. What happens to families when no-fault divorce laws are available, in the opinion of David Blankenhorn, whom the author quotes?
2. What does Rosin say is a more pressing problem than the state of divorce laws?
3. In the author's view, what reforms would make divorce laws fairer to women and children?

From Hanna Rosin, "Separation Anxiety," *New Republic*, May 6, 1995. Reprinted by permission of the *New Republic*, ©1996, The New Republic, Inc.

Since 1993, family values crusaders have been like wandering tribes, fervent and armed but with no place to go. In a euphoric moment after Clinton's election, the tribes united when left-wing communitarians joined their erstwhile conservative foes: a Democratic president declared the answer to poverty was "stable, intact families," and Donna Shalala, parroting the famous *Atlantic Monthly* article, professed that Dan Quayle was right. But the bipartisan convergence deprived both sides of an enemy. "We were lost," sighs David Blankenhorn, from the liberal Institute for American Values. "We had no momentum."

THE EFFECTS OF DIVORCE LAWS

Then in 1996 came a revelation, "like a bolt of lightning," recalls Blankenhorn. The enemy, he and his colleagues realized, was divorce law and, more specifically, "no-fault" divorce reform of the '70s, which allows couples to end their marriage without blame. Instead of having to choose from a menu of sins—adultery, mental cruelty, desertion, imprisonment—no-fault freed a new generation to break up simply because of "irreconcilable differences." "When you change the laws to make divorce quick and easy, you don't need a Ph.D. to know what will happen," he adds. "You'll erode the American family."

Blankenhorn's epiphany sparked a string of conversions. In January 1996, Iowa's Republican governor, Terry Branstad, launched the "Campaign for the Family" and drafted a bill requiring stronger grounds for divorce. Then, on Valentine's Day, a Michigan state representative, Republican Jessie Dalman, introduced a bill overturning the state's no-fault law, arguing that it "cheapens commitment and degrades lifelong love." By April, eighteen states had followed, introducing laws forcing marriage deserters to confess their sin or stick it out. In the meantime, Democrats in Washington turned up the rhetorical heat: in *It Takes a Village*, Hillary Clinton writes that she is "ambivalent about no-fault divorce when children are involved." And her husband agrees, telling congressmen at his national prayer breakfast in February, "It may be that it ought to be a little harder to get a divorce. . . ."

The new divorcephobes accept as an axiom that the no-fault reform wrecked a generation of marriages. "To me, this is like debating whether the earth is round," says Blankenhorn. But the truth is more complicated. The reform may have contributed to a rise in divorce rates—but only compared to the pent-up, atypical '50s. Outside this historical blip, the rate has been steadily climbing since the Civil War, worldwide. The end of marriage begins not with Dr. Benjamin Spock, but with John

Milton, who in his "Doctrine and Discipline of Divorce" declared that without it marriage sours into "drooping and disconsolate household captivity." The more worrisome phenomenon these days is that fewer families form in the first place—a trend that nixing no-fault is likely to encourage by scaring off the already marriage-shy.

THE ANTI-DIVORCE MOVEMENT

How did divorce, once seen as the path to personal happiness, start looking like the seed of America's destruction? The turn begins in the '80s with a defector from the feminist line. When Harvard professor Lenore Weitzman polled 228 women divorced under California's 1969 no-fault statute, she expected to find reduced levels of bitterness and acrimony. Instead, she stumbled on what she called the "new poor," a class of disillusioned women whose incomes had dropped 70 percent after their marriages ended.

Weitzman's portrait of female suffering permanently complicated the easy equation between divorce and women's autonomy, although it's now thought to be exaggerated; the standard figure for income loss has been revised down to 30 percent. It took research on another set of victims—children—to really jumpstart the anti-divorce movement. The study on children most often quoted by divorcephobes is "Growing Up With a Single Parent," published in 1995 by professors Sara McLanahan of Princeton and Gary Sandefur of the University of Wisconsin. The two researchers concluded that, regardless of the race or education of the parents, children who grow up in single-parent homes fare worse at every stage of life: they get lower grades from middle school on and are more likely to drop out of high school; they get worse-paying jobs and are more likely to be unemployed and even to end up in jail. "The evidence is clear," they concluded. "Children who grow up with one parent are definitely worse off."

This research did for the anti-divorce movement what secondhand smoke did for tobaccophobes: it created innocent bystanders. "Children are the quintessential vulnerable citizens. They need and deserve our help," wrote William Galston, Clinton's former domestic policy adviser and an early disciple of the anti-divorce movement. He could now frame the issue in terms only a brute could argue with. "In the end it comes down to a moral question: Is our society willing to put the well-being of children first, even when it may restrain our passion for unfettered autonomy?" What politician could resist? Jessie Dalman's press packet includes a copy of a hand-scrawled letter from a grateful tyke: "Dear Honorable Jessie Dalman, I wanted to write to you and let you know I am supporting you and your stand of divorce reform and I am praying for you. Love, Drew."

Drew may be convinced, but the researchers who interviewed his cohorts are baffled. "That sounds like a bad idea," says Sandefur, when asked about the anti–no-fault movement. "People who get divorced probably should get divorced. The worst thing for kids is to be around a constant state of warfare." McLanahan is equally bewildered. "It's a bit of a sham," she says. "Just an easy fix that will appeal to voters."

To prove no-fault's pernicious influence, the Galstonites rely on a study published in 1995 in the *Journal of Marriage and the Family*, which showed that the divorce rate increased by 15 to 25 percent in the three years following the switch to no-fault in forty-four of the fifty states. But, as Andrew Cherlin, another researcher often cited by Galston, points out, they're missing the first rule of statistics: correlation does not prove causation. The divorce rate has been rising steadily since the 1800s, and it surged in the early '60s—fifteen years before no-fault laws were widespread. The sudden spike in the three years following the reform came from a backlog of cases.

THE DIVORCE-REFORM DEBATE

Like it or not, the country is accustomed to divorce; the only thing squelching no-fault will do is to recreate the sham of another era, when couples who wanted to divorce were obliged to invent affairs and abuse. "In New York, where adultery was the only grounds for divorce, people set up an appointment in a hotel room with a model and a photographer," recalls Herbert Jacob, a professor at Northwestern University who studies divorce. "If the judge wanted mental cruelty, your lawyer would tell you to say he called you names. If the judge wanted physical cruelty, the lawyer would recess, and you'd come back in a few minutes and say he slapped you."

Family boosters balk when they are called retrograde, and even the most conservative among them have learned to defend the reform in feminist terms. "We only want to return justice to marital dissolution," says Kristi Hamrick of the right-wing Family Research Council. "Returning fault gives women a powerful weapon." If the abandoned wife can pin blame on her husband, goes the argument, she can wangle a better settlement. But even this new twist is grounded in Victorian wisdom. "There's a lot of truth in the stereotype," Hamrick continues. "A gentleman decides to change his old wife for a new trophy model, so he writes one check and leaves. Our way gives the woman back some power." In fact, in up to 65 percent of cases, it's the woman who asks to get out of the marriage. And the image of the vulnerable wife rendered helpless by divorce is out of date: in the age group most likely to divorce, 30 percent of women had jobs in 1960; now, three-quarters do.

FIGHT!
FIGHT!
LET ME THROUGH!
FIGHT!
FIGHT!
KIRK
REFORMING NO FAULT DIVORCE

Kirk. Reprinted by permission of Kirk Anderson.

A truly feminist, pro-child divorce reform would look something like this: dock alimony and child support automatically from the sole or primary wage-earner's paycheck, and let whoever has primary custody of the children keep the house. To punish trophy hunters, force them to support the first set of children at the same living standard as the second. This was the radical track Weitzman, who opposed returning to a fault system, suggested in her book and still supports: "Society's views of marriage are reflected in its post-divorce laws," she says. "If we don't reward a mother with alimony, what we are really saying is we don't care about someone dedicating her life to supporting a family."

Since the days of Weitzman's research, state laws have advanced—by splitting pensions, for example, or shaming deadbeat dads. Wisconsin even ensures mothers tax-supported child support. But most states are far behind for what some researchers suspect is a sinister reason: many legislators are divorced men. As Galston points out, the first no-fault statute was drafted by California Assemblyman James Hayes, who divorced his wife of twenty-five years to marry a younger woman. Fourteen of the fifteen people who testified for the law were men; ten were divorced.

DIVORCE AND THE POOR

For Galston, drawing attention to the sins of the overclass is a matter of playing fair, making sure "family values" does not become another way to demonize the poor: "This change is about us, not them," says Galston. But the movement's greatest fault is confounding "us" and "them." In Maggie Gallagher's *The Abolition of Marriage*, there is a chapter describing the author's apocalyptic visions of a "post-marriage" society. It opens with Raphael Rympel, a Haitian schoolboy shot dead in the playground. This happened in Crown Heights, but "there is no escape from Crown Heights," Gallagher writes, "because every neighborhood in America is just like it," by which she means that every neighborhood in America is an open sore left by divorce culture. The poor children there are no worse off than Melissa, a smart and pretty pre-law student who, as a child of divorce, is haunted by fears of abandonment. "Even most concentration camp survivors grow up to be law-abiding citizens," Gallagher memorably puts it, explaining why outward success is deceptive.

To show that divorce doesn't discriminate, Gallagher cites a well-known study by Judith Wallerstein, in which sixty mostly affluent California families were tracked for ten years. Only one-third of the divorced dads chose to pay for their children's college; 60 percent of the children did worse in school than their fathers. If these white, educated, upper-middle-class children can't hack it, Gallagher suggests, just imagine what happens to the black and poor. She seems to forget that it's only in white, middle-class America that too much anxiety seems as bad as too little money. Comparing the two is like saying if Woody Allen can't keep his family together, imagine what will happen to the rest of us.

It's hard to imagine the family faithfuls really believe that changing divorce law is the best they can do for the Raphael Rympels of this world. At least for the politicians of the movement, dragging the Rympels into the debate is useful for other reasons. Governor Branstad of Iowa began our conversation by citing the usual litany of doomsday statistics: "Poverty, drug abuse, juvenile delinquency, the crime rate, are all associated with the breakup of the traditional family." But in his "Campaign for the Family" it's not the juveniles he is concerned about. "If a child grows up angry in a broken home and feels like nobody loves them, it's likely they'll become a drug addict and rob you."

And, if it's not the underclass he's worried about, Branstad can rest easy. There's been a yuppie stampede to America's altars: a 1993 University of Pennsylvania study found female college graduates were marrying younger than they did in the '70s. We've always been the most marriage-happy Western country, and lately we've started to celebrate it with a vengeance. In movies, books and syrupy newspaper features, America is suddenly awash in nuptial splendor. Screen hits of the '70s celebrating wives unshackled by divorce—*An Unmarried Woman, Kramer vs. Kramer*—have been replaced by parables of couples who stick together through affairs, alcoholism and streams of verbal abuse: *Flirting with Disaster, Something to Talk About, When a Man Loves a Woman, Leaving Las Vegas*, "Married With Children." In bookstores, *The Creative Divorce*, a best-seller of the divorce decade, has been superseded by *The Good Marriage*, Judith Wallerstein's book of secrets to making love last.

It's a shift the Galstonites, in their self-styled Jeremiad pose, recognize. "The people of your generation, the children of divorce, are displaying a yearning for restabilization," Galston explains. "Faced with the reality of divorce, Generation X is expressing the ardent hope that 'This won't happen to me.'" Then, pausing for a sip of coffee, he lets me in on the cosmic secret: "Sociologists think this might be the Great Awakening."

| "Divorces in non-abusive cases have a negative effect on children in a number of key areas: school performance; psychological illness; crime; suicide."

NO-FAULT DIVORCE LAWS HAVE HARMED CHILDREN

William A. Galston

The passage of no-fault divorce laws beginning in the late 1960s has created a climate in which divorce has flourished, asserts William A. Galston. Galston, a professor at the University of Maryland and a former domestic policy assistant to President Bill Clinton, argues that this increase in the divorce rate has resulted in numerous social and psychological problems for the children of divorced parents. He contends that returning to a fault-based system for couples with minor children would reduce the number of divorces and prevent many of the social pathologies that afflict the children of the United States.

As you read, consider the following questions:

1. How much did the divorce rate increase between 1960 and 1980, according to the author?
2. In Galston's opinion, what are the three points at which divorces involving minor children can be reduced?

From William A. Galston, "Braking Divorce for the Sake of Children," *American Enterprise*, May/June 1996. Reprinted by permission of the *American Enterprise*, a Washington, D.C.- based magazine of politics, business, and culture.

How would we alter the law and practice of divorce in the United States if we were truly guided by the best interests of children?

We have good reason to be worried about the current state of marriage and divorce in this country, and the implications for the young. Between 1960 and 1980, the U.S. divorce rate surged by nearly 250 percent. It has since leveled off at a rate that is by far the highest in the industrialized world. About half of all marriages undertaken today will end in divorce.

THE EFFECT OF DIVORCE ON CHILDREN

Since the 1960s, the number of children directly touched by divorce has jumped from 485,000 to one million a year. The percentage of children living in mother-only households has more than doubled, and about 40 percent of such children have not seen their fathers during the past year.

Research suggests that where there has been physical abuse or extreme emotional cruelty, a divorce can be less harmful for children than if the parents had remained married. But where divorce follows lower-intensity conflict—and this covers at least half of all divorces—most children will be much better off if the marriage is maintained. Even after correcting for the effects of pre-divorce conflict and income loss after divorce, it becomes clear that divorces in non-abusive cases have a negative effect on children in a number of key areas: school performance; psychological illness; crime; suicide; out-of-wedlock births; adult work performance; and the propensity to become divorced. There is also evidence that the experience of divorce diminishes trust in people and institutions, and impedes the capacity of individuals to form stable, lasting relationships.

NO-FAULT DIVORCE

As recently as 30 years ago, every state had fault-based divorce laws. The standard grounds for divorce included adultery, physical abuse, mental cruelty, desertion, imprisonment, addiction, and insanity. The first no-fault divorce statute was signed into law by then-Governor Ronald Reagan of California in late 1969. By 1974, 45 states had adopted some form of no-fault.

Evidence is accumulating that no-fault laws themselves accelerated the pace of divorce. A 50-state survey recently published in the *Journal of Marriage and the Family* concluded that "the switch from fault divorce law to no-fault divorce law led to a measurable increase in the divorce rate." Legal changes coincided with economic and cultural shifts. Compared to 30 years ago, Daniel

Yankelovich finds, today's Americans place less value on obligation to others, on sacrifice, and on self-restraint. We place more value on individualism, on self-expression, and on personal choice.

A result is that we are far more accepting of divorce than we were 30 years ago. We are far more likely to say that marriage is first and foremost a means to personal happiness. And we are far less inclined to believe that parents in a less than fully satisfactory marriage ought to make an effort to stay together for the sake of their children. Up to the early-1960s, more than half of Americans thought that parents had an obligation to make this effort. By the 1990s, that figure had declined to less than one-fifth.

ONE SIMPLE GOAL

American society may never return to the low divorce rates of the nineteenth century. But surely it is possible, as a first step, to achieve one simple goal: to create a society in which more marriages succeed than fail and in which each year more children (rather than fewer) are born into the relative safety of marriage.

Maggie Gallagher, Insight, April 15, 1996.

There are three points at which we may be able to reduce divorces involving minor children. The first occurs at or before the threshold of marriage. It is stunning how many schools talk about sex while failing to discuss marriage in any sustained manner. It is a legitimate function of public education to treat marriage seriously as a human and social institution. Religious institutions also ought to intervene more often to support marriage. If every church and synagogue took as one of its principal tasks the thorough preparation of young people for marriage, it could make a significant difference. There is evidence that this strategy works best when all the religious institutions within a community unite around this objective in a mutually reinforcing way.

The second point of intervention occurs during marriage. At a minimum, we should systematically re-examine our economic and social policies (and our tax code) with an eye to creating a marriage-friendly environment. In addition, religious institutions should offer programs for couples who want to renew their vows or confront problems that could lead to marital dissolution if left unaddressed.

The third key point of intervention occurs at the threshold of divorce. We should institute significant changes in the current regime of no-fault divorce laws, in effect creating a two-tier system. For couples without minor children, current law can be left in place. For couples with minor children, we should eliminate unilateral no-fault—where one person can readily obtain a divorce without the other's consent—and return to an updated fault system, with the alternative of a five-year waiting period. And even in cases where both parties consent, there should be suitable braking mechanisms: mandatory pause of at least a year for reflection, counseling, and mediation.

Is our society willing to put the well-being of children first, even when it may conflict with adult desires? The next generation will decide how well we have answered this question, and they will judge us accordingly.

"Divorce-reform battles were fought in the sixties . . . because society saw the devastating effects of fault-based divorce laws on children and families."

NO-FAULT DIVORCE LAWS HAVE NOT HARMED CHILDREN

Constance Ahrons

Sociology professor Constance Ahrons directs the marriage and family-therapy program at the University of Southern California and is the author of *The Good Divorce*. In the following viewpoint, Ahrons disputes the contention that no-fault divorce has harmed children. She insists that the fault-based system of the past was harmful to children because it involved a long, combative process that encouraged acrimony between divorcing couples. No-fault divorce, on the other hand, allows parents to provide a co-operative environment for their children during the divorce process.

As you read, consider the following questions:

1. What does Ahrons mean when she says that "'The Family' has become the national scapegoat"?
2. According to the author, what problems do reformers associate with single-parent families?
3. What does no-fault divorce do for children, according to the author?

From Constance Ahrons, "Trying to Turn Back the Clock Won't Meet the Needs of Families," *Insight*, April 15, 1996. Reprinted by permission of *Insight*. Copyright 1996 by News World Communications, Inc. All rights reserved.

The highly publicized finding that living in a single-parent family is disadvantageous to children and their mothers is a major focal point in the increasingly heated "family values" debate. This finding quickly translates into the conclusion that the nuclear family is the sole unit acceptable for healthy child rearing. The solution then becomes that government needs to intervene with laws that are punitive toward all non-nuclear families: cut welfare, make divorce laws harsher, create incentives for marriage, stigmatize single parents and homosexuals and close sperm banks.

FAMILY-BASHING

Well, it's not a surprise and it's not new. It's *family-bashing* time again. When politicians can't find solutions to inadequate and inequitable wage and job structures, a seriously troubled education system and a woefully underfunded health-care system, they point their fingers at the smallest, most-vulnerable system in society. "The Family" has become the national scapegoat.

The politicians' prescription is simple: Get married, stay married and be good parents. In this current political ploy to label marriage as the antidote to society's problems, the suggested cure is: Promote the two-parent family as the salvation of our children; make divorce more difficult; reinstate fault-based laws. This glib rhetoric diverts attention and draws people into a conspiracy of silence about the real issues. That isn't to say that families aren't in trouble; indeed they are. But the reason is not that society is becoming antifamily, as the traditionalists proclaim. Families are in trouble because American culture and American leaders cling to an outdated ideal of the traditional nuclear family. This prevents the creation of necessary policies and economic structures to support the real families that make up today's society.

Real families—in all their ethnic, class, gender and structural differences such as single-parent, dual-worker, binuclear, remarried and homosexual—far outnumber traditional nuclear families in today's society. But too many politicians and conservative thinkers glorify and reinforce a destructive mythology that stigmatizes non-nuclear families and ignores the realities of family life in the nineties. For example, consider the very basic value of loving and unconditionally protecting children. So many people hold this dear, yet society routinely fails to meet the needs of children. Why is it that America claims to cherish its children yet pays schoolteachers and day-care workers extremely low wages? School systems are in big trouble; day care is grossly underfunded. Why—until President Clinton's election—has the

United States been the only industrialized country in the Western world without a national parental-leave policy? It still lags far behind other countries, providing as it does only unpaid leave. Policies that would support parenting, such as flextime, on-site day care and paid family leave, are rare.

AMERICANS DO NOT VALUE CHILDREN

The current economy, with high unemployment and an alarmingly high incidence of poverty, and the conservative political climate, with the decrease in governmental support to institutions that serve children and families, have exacerbated the problems. Americans can talk idealistically and abstractly, but the reality is that they don't place a high value on children.

Waving the banner of family values will not improve the welfare of children. Whether they have one, two, three or four parents, children still require the support of their communities and their government.

REFORMS MAY MAKE DIVORCE WORSE

It is fair to say that we have spent too little time thinking of public policies to support marriage. But there's no reason to believe that making divorce harder will make marriage easier.

For one thing, we don't know if no-fault divorce was the cause or the by-product of rising divorce rates. That's still under debate. For another thing, older divorced women don't do any better financially in a state without unilateral no-fault, such as New York, than in states with it.

There is no certainty that changing the rules will prevent "frivolous divorces." But it could turn "good divorces" bad. A longer waiting period might postpone a quick remarriage. But we have no idea if it would prevent divorce.

A return to those wonderful yesteryears of legal wrangle and rancor might well be worse for children. Let's remember the one area in which divorcing parents are still required to place blame: custody disputes. Not a pretty model.

Ellen Goodman, ©1996, The Boston Globe Newspaper Co./Washington Post Writers Group. Reprinted with permission.

Ever since former Vice President Dan Quayle made his famous attack on Murphy Brown, single-parent families have been at the center of the family-values debate. That children in single-parent families do not fare as well as children living with both biological parents is a highly publicized finding. But what, really, are the disadvantages? Single-parent families have lower incomes;

the parents have less time to spend with their children; and they have less access to community resources. Instead of marshaling remedies to these real needs, conservative politicians, the "moral majority" and the religious right want to blame the victims, stigmatize non-nuclear families and add to their burdens.

Take a closer look at the overly popularized and simplified finding concerning children of single-parent families. The variables of gender, race and class are central to any interpretation of the data. Single-parent families are poor because 90 percent are headed by women and a large proportion are nonwhite. Given these demographic facts, who would expect their income levels to be equal to two-parent white households? The underlying contextual variables of poverty, racism and sexism are far more important in interpreting the data than whether there are one or two biological parents in the household. Other studies, smaller in sample size but using a more complex model of family structures, have not found differences in child adjustment based upon family structure alone.

THE NUCLEAR FAMILY

When the traditionalists bemoan the demise of The Family, they are referring to the nuclear family—and blame for the collapse of one of America's most treasured institutions usually is placed on women. Concerns about child care are seen as women's problems. Working mothers are rapped as the cause of problems associated with latchkey children, drugs and delinquency. Rarely is anyone heard talking about the problem of working fathers, nor does one hear proposals for a "daddy track." Women still carry major responsibilities for home and family even when they share equally in the economic support. Current research documents this and with it the accompanying stress experienced by women in dual-earner families.

Rather than working on reforms to mitigate the greater societal problems that undermine the quality of life for all of America's families, irrespective of their form, the traditionalists plead for a return to the family of yesteryear. Although political correctness keeps politicians from stating it overtly, it is suggested covertly that what children in these two-parent nuclear families need is to be cared for by full-time mothers. Not only do economics prohibit this, but also history has taught that it is detrimental to women on a number of different levels.

By far, the biggest culprit in this zealous mission to preserve marriage as a lifelong commitment is the fact that almost half of married couples are divorced. It's not that they don't like marriage. In fact, it's quite the opposite. The vast majority of men and women who divorce will remarry. And many of those like the institution so well that they may even do it a third or fourth time.

Divorce-reform battles were fought in the sixties—the era that is cast in dark, evil shadows—because society saw the devastating effects of fault-based divorce laws on children and families. Opponents of no-fault divorce fail to understand that litigation hurts kids. When one spouse must prove the other to be "at fault," divorce becomes a pitched battle between adversaries who each must prove the other committed adultery, spousal abuse or child abuse or destroyed the home. It's the *War of the Roses* all over again. Anger escalates and continues for years or decades following the divorce. Not only are the spouses angry at each other for the perceived injustices of the marriage, but added to this are the new assaults required by the fault-based divorce proceedings.

CHILDREN ARE HOSTAGES

And what happens to the children? They are held hostages in a long, vicious war, watching their parents duel it out. This public battle occurs at the expense of the children. The wait for a resolution is itself harmful: Crowded court schedules force divorcing parents to wait in line, first to get a place on the docket and then later, physically, at court. It's common to see hallways filled with parents waiting their turn as the lawyers' fees mount sky-high. It's the family who pays for the lawyers, psychologists, private investigators and accountants who form the industry of fault-based divorce. What a wasteful allocation of the family's resources. As one of my research subjects sighed, "The money was used to put our lawyers' children through college instead of our own kids."

Opponents of no-fault are quick to pull out statistics that show divorce leaves disturbed children in its wake. This simplistic conclusion is inaccurate and misleading—a sound bite extracted from a large body of research. It is irresponsible to state the findings from one study as fact, irrespective of the methodology. What the research shows is that when children continue to have postdivorce relationships with emotionally healthy parents and when the parents do not embroil the children in their conflicts, these children show no long-term psychological damage. But bad news makes headlines; good news is boring.

At the heart of no-fault legislation is that children need parents, during marriage or divorce, who are nurturing and responsible. No-fault reduces the acrimony; parents are helped to find suitable ways to fulfill their responsibilities. Teaching divorcing parents problem-solving and dispute-resolution skills helps families of divorce more than mudslinging.

Another important fact is that many of the negative effects on children pre-date the divorce. Loveless marriages, parental depression and emotional distance leave emotional scars that continue through adulthood. Children from intact high-conflict homes fare worse in the long run than do children of divorce.

A CIVILIZED ARENA

Although no-fault legislation is far from perfect, it does provide a civilized arena in which marriage can be terminated while parents continue to be parents. Yes, society needs to solve the economic problems of female-led households and, yes, fathers need to stay emotionally involved with and financially responsible for their children. But bringing fault back into divorce legislation will not solve these problems. It will create other, worse problems.

It's ludicrous to think we can legislate happy marriages by making divorce more punitive. Let's ask former Senate Majority Leader Bob Dole and House Speaker Newt Gingrich if they wish they'd been prevented by law from ending their first marriages. Let's ask them if they—and their children—would prefer the first marriage to have remained intact. And let's ask their former spouses and current wives—and their children—what result this would have had on The Family.

Periodical Bibliography

The following articles have been selected to supplement the diverse views presented in this chapter. Addresses are provided for periodicals not indexed in the *Readers' Guide to Periodical Literature*, the *Alternative Press Index*, the *Social Sciences Index*, or the *Index to Legal Periodicals and Books*.

Joseph Adelson	"Splitting Up," *Commentary*, September 1996.
Andrew J. Cherlin	"Nostalgia as Family Policy," *Public Interest*, Winter 1993.
Hillary R. Clinton	"Divorce and the Effect on Children," *Liberal Opinion Week*, February 5, 1996. Available from Living History, Inc., 108 E. Fifth St., Vinton, IA 52349.
Barbara Ehrenreich	"In Defense of Splitting Up," *Time*, April 8, 1996.
Susan Faludi	"Statistically Challenged," *Nation*, April 15, 1996.
Martha Albertson Fineman	"Icon of Marriage Has Had Its Day," *Insight*, June 27, 1994. Available from 3600 New York Ave. NE, Washington, DC 20002.
Maggie Gallagher	"Yes, Welfare Reform and Tax Incentives Can Reverse the Anti-Marriage Tilt," *Insight*, April 15, 1996.
John Gottman	"Why Marriages Fail," *Family Therapy Networker*, May/June 1994. Available from 8528 Bradford Rd., Silver Spring, MD 20901.
John Leland	"Tightening the Knot," *Newsweek*, February 19, 1996.
Laura Mansnerus	"The Divorce Backlash," *Working Woman*, February 1995.
Robert L. Plunkett	"Vow for Now," *National Review*, May 29, 1995.
Glenn T. Stanton	"The Counter-Revolution Against Easy Divorce," *American Enterprise*, May/June 1996. Available from PO Box 2013, Marion, OH 43305-2013.
David M. Wagner	"Time to Roll Back No-Fault Divorce," *Insight*, June 27, 1994.
Barbara Dafoe Whitehead	"Without Marriage as a Bridge, the Male-Female Divide Becomes a Chasm," *American Enterprise*, May/June 1996.

CHAPTER 3

HOW DO WORK-RELATED POLICIES AFFECT THE FAMILY?

Chapter Preface

Cindy, a married mother of two profiled by journalist Patricia Hedberg in a 1996 *Business Ethics* article, worked as an accountant in a busy Boston firm. Each weekday, she faced a stressful forty-five-minute drive to her office where her hours were filled with exacting, demanding work. Because she usually did not return home until mid-evening, she hired workers to pick up her children at school, shop for groceries, and prepare dinner. After years of this schedule, however, Cindy felt exhausted, irritable, and concerned about how little time she spent with her family. Finally she and her husband decided to sell their home and move to Syracuse, New York, to find new jobs. Cindy found a part-time job with a company that allowed her to work at home. "Though [the couple's] new income is less than one-third of what they collectively earned in Boston," states Hedberg, "Cindy's life is far more manageable and enjoyable."

Many workers with families appreciate "family-friendly" employers like Cindy's who offer flexible work options and benefits such as part-time hours, job sharing, telecommuting, parental leave, and day care. These workers welcome the opportunity to rearrange their work lives so that they can have more time and energy for their families.

However, opponents of family-oriented work programs contend that the policies are not always as flexible or as fair as they appear to be. Syndicated columnist Suzanne Fields points out that "childless women not only resent paycheck deductions for day care and maternity benefits for others when they'd rather have the benefits of higher salaries or longer vacations, but they're beginning to suspect that they're singled out—discriminated against—for undesirable transfers, overtime and more inflexible tasks." Moreover, some workers maintain that family-related work issues are personal and should not be managed through companywide programs. John Goodwin, a human-resources manager for a midwestern energy company, argues that "family issues should . . . be worked out independently, not as a matter of company policy, so that differences of 'lifestyle' and age can be personalized."

Balancing work and home life is just one of the dilemmas modern families face in a shifting economy. The authors in the following chapter offer various opinions on this much-discussed issue.

| "It is very encouraging that many corporations and businesses are realizing the advantages of adopting 'family-friendly' policies."

FAMILY-FRIENDLY CORPORATE POLICIES ARE BENEFICIAL

Joseph Bernardin

Some corporations have instituted "family-friendly" policies—including health care insurance, parental leave, family counseling, flexible work hours, and day care—in an attempt to increase productivity while fostering employee morale and family life. In the following viewpoint, excerpted from a speech delivered before the National Conference of Christians and Jews in June 1996, Joseph Bernardin contends that companies that offer such policies help to strengthen the family. Before his death in November 1996, Bernardin was the Cardinal archbishop of the Roman Catholic Archdiocese of Chicago.

As you read, consider the following questions:

1. What are some of corporate America's ethical problems, according to Bernardin?
2. According to the author, what happened to football player David Williams when he missed a game because of the birth of his child?
3. Which ethical principles should guide corporate America, in Bernardin's opinion?

Joseph Bernardin, "Ethics in Corporate America: Formula for Success," *America*, July 6, 1996. Reprinted with permission.

I have been asked to address you this evening on a formula for success in regard to ethics in corporate America. May I begin by stating the obvious: I stand before you as a pastor. What do I know about the corporate world, other than having many close friends who have devoted their lives to that environment?

Well, I am also the C.E.O. of a relatively large corporation—the Archdiocese of Chicago, which is totally dependent on free-will offerings and has experienced many financial difficulties through the years but is expected, nonetheless, to educate tens of thousands of children, both rich and poor, provide a wide range of social services to more than a half-million people each year, pay just wages to its over 18,000 employees and always have patience, understanding, compassion and good humor. As you can imagine, it's quite a challenge!

So, in a very real sense, while our calls are different, you who are C.E.O.'s or managers and I experience many of the same realities and challenges. As a pastoral leader, I must also give close personal attention to the ethical problems, challenges and dilemmas that my colleagues and I face in managing the vast resources of this local church.

CORPORATE AMERICA'S ETHICAL PROBLEMS

Before we attempt to articulate a formula for success in regard to ethical issues, we must ask: What are the ethical problems, dilemmas and challenges facing corporate America today? While news stories and features highlight many of them, I will mention only a few. You undoubtedly have your own personal lists of ethical concerns.

Some of the ethical issues are obviously unethical: unfair hiring practices, dishonest business practices, unfair labor practices, deceptive advertising, unjust compensation of workers. Businesses that engage in such endeavors apparently set their goals on short-term gains at the risk of long-term losses, to say nothing of extensive litigation.

Other dilemmas arise in the highly competitive, globally interdependent world market in which much business is conducted today. Examples include downsizing the workforce and increasing the workloads of remaining workers in order to compete more effectively, outsourcing work to avoid paying costly benefits to members of labor unions and shifting production to much cheaper labor markets overseas. The question that arises, naturally, is: What happens to the workers who are laid off, terminated or displaced? What happens to their families? What happens to their dreams, their self-esteem, their ability to cope with the pressures of contemporary life?

Still other ethical issues that have long been part of the scene in corporate America seem to have been exacerbated in recent years. One thinks, for instance, of ineffective personnel policies regarding issues like sexual harassment and racial or gender discrimination, little or no commitment by a corporation to the broader community, the attitude that the end justifies the means and an "ethic" that insists that work should be the number one priority in a person's life, second to none—that a company's bottom line is all that matters.

In mentioning these problems, I am not implying that all corporations and businesses engage in them. There are many that are run both ethically and compassionately. Indeed, when others do not act this way, it is an embarrassment to those that are guided by ethical and humane considerations.

None of these issues is one-sided or one-dimensional. Each involves many financial, strategic, corporate and socio-political considerations. But they also have ethical dimensions because of their impact on human lives.

FAMILY SHOULD TAKE PRIORITY

To highlight what I mean, let us consider what may seem like a less obvious ethical challenge to corporate America today. In 1993, Houston Oilers tackle David Williams missed his team's game in Boston because he stayed in Houston to be with his wife during the birth of their first child. The Oilers fined him one week's salary ($111,111) and threatened to suspend him. Since Williams's wife had earlier suffered an ectopic pregnancy, he had decided to be with her as she gave birth, despite relentless pleas from his coaches to take the next plane to Boston.

Most people were outraged by the Oilers' actions, but some defended them. One coach even compared Williams's decision to miss the game to missing action in World War II! Fortunately, few people would equate a football game with a major world war, nor would most willingly let work responsibilities take precedence over a once-in-a-lifetime family experience.

Whether it is a joyous occasion like the birth of a child or a traumatic situation like a child's life-threatening illness, there are times when one's family takes priority over other pressing matters. And today, when so many families are hurting deeply, you and I, as leaders in business, labor, government and the church or synagogue, should not and cannot afford to ignore family life realities. They consistently come back to haunt us in terms of lost productivity, the erosion of the social order and costly social problems spawned by the instability of family life.

The threat of downsizing and unemployment, inadequate educational opportunities, domestic violence and many other problems can overwhelm parents who struggle to provide adequate food, shelter, safety and security for their families. Indeed, today many families struggle against economic, social, moral and cultural forces that undermine healthy family life. One of these forces is the investment of much time and energy—often by both parents—to earn an adequate living for their family. As a result, the average parent spends 40 percent less time with his or her children today than he or she did 20 years ago. While social institutions increasingly share many of the family's responsibilities toward children, they can never take the place of families.

THE BENEFITS OF WORK-FAMILY PROGRAMS

To get the most out of progressive work-family policies, companies must change their culture as well as their practices. So suggests a 1993 study by the Families and Work Institute documenting the effect of a series of work-family programs introduced by pharmaceuticals giant Johnson & Johnson (J&J) in 1989. Two years after J&J began offering on-site child care, flexible work arrangements, resource-and-referral services and management training on work-family practices, employees reported a sharp increase in the supportiveness of their supervisors. Employees with supportive bosses also experienced less job interference with their family lives and were likelier to recommend the company as a place to work.

Julia Lawlor, *Working Woman*, July/August 1996.

It is very encouraging that many corporations and businesses are realizing the advantages of adopting "family-friendly" policies. I commend those corporations that are developing innovative programs and policies that help to support family life. Take, for instance, health care and life insurance benefits, employee assistance programs, flexible work policies and options like flexible work time, compressed work weeks, job sharing, telecommuting and home-based employment, maternal and paternal leave, day care and leave-banks of sick time for employees facing catastrophic illnesses.

As you and I know, becoming "family-friendly" and supportive of employees in times of family crises involves much more than changing personnel policies and educating people about how to deal with stress, substance abuse or other difficulties. We must learn to view everything we do through a "family prism." This means changing attitudes, shifting emphases, engendering a philosophy and creating a climate that underscores the importance of the family so that it permeates everything we do.

To bring this about, my friends, must we not start with our own lives? Are our employees the only ones who find it difficult to integrate work and family life today, particularly during a time of stress? What about us managers? As leaders, must we not first evaluate our own lives?

EMPLOYEES DESERVE RESPECT

Once we have done this, it is important that we look at our employees not simply as people who work for us, but as individuals with needs and dreams, problems and potential. Employees are a long-term resource in which you and I have a substantial investment. As we become more sensitive to their personal needs and respect them as fellow citizens and valuable contributors to society, we will discover that they are indeed our brothers and sisters before God!

When we look upon our co-workers with such respect, we have begun to integrate a vital moral or ethical dimension into our management style, policies and decisions. Another key ingredient in such an ethical vision is concern for the common good, which can be defined as "the sum total of social conditions that allow people, either as groups or as individuals, to reach their fulfillment more fully and easily."

These two convictions—about the dignity of each human life and the necessity of working for the common good of society—form the bedrock of Catholic social teaching. They also pose three key ethical questions for corporate America (including the church itself): 1) What do our policies and decisions do for our people—our employees, our clients or consumers, our community? 2) What do our policies and decisions do to our people? 3) How do our people participate in the development of our policies and decisions?

BASIC ETHICAL PRINCIPLES

It is no secret that, although some people derive great benefit from corporate policies and decisions, others are neglected. The lives of some are greatly enhanced, while many others experience a tragic devaluing as they sink deeper into the mire of poverty and are forced to live in subhuman conditions. Moreover, a few make all or most of the economic decisions, while the vast majority remain voiceless and powerless.

Certain basic ethical principles need to shape our vision of corporate America. In particular, I propose for your consideration two that derive from what I have just said:

- While the economic dimension must surely be considered, corporate economic policies and decisions should also be judged in the light of whether they protect or undermine the dignity of the human persons affected—workers and their families, clients or consumers and the citizens of the community.
- Employees should be given an opportunity to participate in the development of corporate policies and decisions that affect their lives. Participation can be implemented in many ways: through consultation, labor negotiations, employee councils, listening sessions, focus groups, town hall meetings.

A Moral Vision for Corporate America

Some claim that corporations cannot afford to be fully ethical, let alone "family-friendly," in their business policies and practices. I disagree. Recent studies of major corporations show that helping employees with family conflicts or difficulties boosts morale and increases productivity. In fact, responding to people in times of need makes good business sense. Besides, when workers are threatened constantly by downsizing and possible unemployment, how can we expect them to concentrate fully on their work, let alone develop any sense of loyalty to their company?

In the long run, taking into consideration the common good of our society will eventually produce huge dividends for all of us in terms of fewer costly social problems. It will also enable the near-poor, the poor and the growing underclass to become more productive workers and citizens as well as consumers. More importantly, by respecting the worker as a person and working for the common good, we will be carrying out our ethical responsibilities and doing God's work on earth.

"Increasingly, . . . workers without young children are feeling exploited."

FAMILY-FRIENDLY CORPORATE POLICIES CAN BE COUNTERPRODUCTIVE

Laurie M. Grossman

In the following viewpoint, Laurie M. Grossman argues that childless workers receive unfair treatment from companies that have adopted "family-friendly" policies. Such policies—which are intended to accommodate employees who have difficulties balancing work and family life—often require childless employees to work longer hours and relocate more often than employees who have children, Grossman maintains. She contends that companies should offer employee-support programs that benefit childless workers as well as workers with children. Grossman is a staff reporter for the *Wall Street Journal*.

As you read, consider the following questions:

1. According to Grossman, how many U.S. workers do not have any children under age eighteen?
2. Why does James Finkelstein resent working at his office on weekends, according to the author?
3. What has Spiegel, Inc., done to support childless employees as well as employees with children?

As the adage says: No good deed goes unpunished.

Just ask the folks at Corning Inc. The Corning, N.Y., optical-fiber and ceramic-products company went all out to help the families of its employees, paying for child-care programs and for counseling on care for elderly relatives. But the efforts made some Corning workers angry.

"After the first couple of years, people who didn't have young children started quietly saying, 'What about us? Does my personal life count?'" recalls Sonia Werner, a work/life balance consultant at Corning. Then, at some open meetings about benefits, the childless spoke up. Ms. Werner says they told management it was unfair "to overemphasize child-care issues to the detriment of single people, to say singles should be married to the company."

Resentment Among Childless Workers

As many companies try harder to accommodate employees with families, they may inadvertently create resentment among childless workers. Nearly two-thirds of U.S. workers don't have any children under age 18. And increasingly, research shows, these workers without young children are feeling exploited.

The list of grievances is long. Many childless workers complain that they're expected to work more hours than their counterparts who have children. Some lament having been transferred more often, and still others resent having to forfeit more weekends.

During the work day, childless workers say they frequently have to answer the phones and absorb extra work to cover for parents who arrive late or leave early to deliver or retrieve children. Many also feel they lose out in benefit packages that favor families with children.

Too often, these employees believe, the children are used as a convenient cop-out. Julie Miller, an advertising copy writer in St. Louis, says she resents being pressured to volunteer for local marketing groups after hours, while other workers beg off "to fix dinner for the kids." Dorothy Lawicki, a hospital nurse in Atlanta, gets angry because other employees with sick children frequently flee in the middle of the work shift, leaving her with extra patients to tend. Kimberly Allen, an internal-audit director in Deerfield, Ill., despises all the typing she must do nearly every week because of a secretary's persistent absences for child-related reasons.

In general, childless employees are annoyed when they aren't given the same flexibility or latitude. "If you don't have kids, it's assumed you don't have a life outside the office," complains Lori DeWeerd, a secretary in Chicago. "Your free time isn't respected." Diane Mills, a flight attendant based in San Francisco, felt obliged to lie to her employer by calling in sick so she could care for her grandmother who broke a hip. For childless employees, she says, asking for time off in such instances is treated "like a demerit."

Such experiences and attitudes aren't isolated. According to recent surveys of about 14,000 workers by Hewitt Associates, an employee-benefits consultant in Lincolnshire, Ill., about 20% of employees complain that co-workers with children are unfairly singled out for help. "Parents in the workplace are the ones getting all the sympathy from the boss," contends Leslie Lafayette, a high-school English teacher in suburban Sacramento, Calif.

In the summer of 1992, Ms. Lafayette started a support group called Childfree Network that aims to redress what it views as workplace inequities. The group has attracted more than 2,000 members in about 50 chapters around the country, and Ms. Lafayette now publishes a quarterly newsletter. No Kidding, a similar group founded by Jerry Steinberg in Vancouver, British Columbia, now boasts about 140 members in the U.S.

These initiatives may be symptoms of a deeper schism. In many workplaces, experts say, bitterness simmers just below the surface. Phyllis Moen, professor of sociology and human development at Cornell University in Ithaca, N.Y., warns of the emergence of "two classes of workers." She suggests that employees with children constitute an increasingly privileged category. At the same time, more and more childless employees seethe with resentment about subtle forms of discrimination.

FACES OF UNFAIRNESS

In response, a few companies have started to make amends. But most employers still haven't addressed the concerns of childless employees, and hard feelings abound. To those who feel victimized, the unfairness has several dimensions. Consider the experiences of these typical workers who have no children:

• Patricia Molloy, a 36-year-old administrative assistant at a large consumer-products company, says she often stays two hours late to put together mailings for shareholders, while others in the office leave to pick up their children. In 1992, after a late-mailing episode, she didn't get home on her birthday until about 9 p.m., two hours too late for her reservations at a favorite local restaurant.

Mrs. Molloy's husband, a fitness trainer, usually eats dinner alone. That pattern often spoils the end of the day for her. "It causes tension at home when he hears the boss left earlier and we were stuck in the office," she says. "It does get him angry, and that upsets me."

• James Finkelstein, an administrator at George Mason University in Fairfax, Va., figures he spends two to five weekend days a month in the office, and usually he's the only one there. Mr. Finkelstein and his wife, a psychological counselor, have little chance to spend time together during the work week, so their weekends are precious.

But his weekend plans often have been spoiled because current or former colleagues would "carve out and jealously protect time with their children, especially on weekends," he says. For example, his wife has to go to museums and movies alone or with friends because he's stuck on campus. "It bothers her more than it bothers me, but it still bothers me," he says.

The 40-year-old Mr. Finkelstein also regrets having missed spending time on weekends with friends from Switzerland and Israel who came to visit the couple. "I haven't been as good a host as I would like to be," he says.

Discrimination Against Childless Women

Childless women not only resent paycheck deductions for day care and maternity benefits for others when they'd rather have the benefits of higher salaries or longer vacations, but they're beginning to suspect that they're singled out—discriminated against—for undesirable transfers, overtime and more inflexible tasks.

Suzanne Fields, *Conservative Chronicle*, July 7, 1993.

• Susan Pisani, a 35-year-old marketing-services director for a unit of ITT Corp., wanted to drive three hours from her St. Louis office to be with her parents for Christmas. But during holiday periods, she says her office defers to families with children. "Someone has to be here to run the office, and it's usually the people who don't have kids who end up staying," she says. "I stayed and picked up the slack."

On Christmas Eve, she worked until 3 p.m., long after others had disappeared. Her parents, in their 70s, made the long drive to stay with her for the holiday. But her condominium was so small that they had to stay in a hotel. And both parents had come down with the flu, which worsened during the trip. So, after being in town less than 24 hours, the parents shared a quick Christmas breakfast with their daughter and son-in-law and then drove straight home.

Many childless workers also believe they are readier targets when it comes to transfers. Sometimes they are asked to pull up stakes and go on a moment's notice.

"You're more eligible for foreign assignments than if you have children. It's cheaper, quicker and also more lonely," says Jeffrey Hansen, a national project manager at the financial-services unit of Household International Inc., in Prospect Heights, Ill. He is spending two years on assignment in Sydney, Australia, after flying out on a Friday and starting work the following Monday.

Carol Kiryluk was transferred eight times during her 19 years with a major oil company. Often, she was moved mere weeks after the subject of a transfer had been broached, while families with children would get more time to adjust. "The uprooting process for me was more abrupt," she says, and resettling became "a solitary burden" that wasn't easy. After the fifth or sixth move, she saw her colleagues with children staying put.

The experience, she now believes, greatly affected her personal life and may even have hurt her own chances to start a family. Ms. Kiryluk canceled her long-anticipated trip to the Galapagos and Machu Picchu for a sudden transfer and gave up many a weekend hiking trip for work. With so many transfers and with friendships abruptly cut off, she says she hesitated to form close relationships. And she felt isolated from social gatherings intended for couples or families from the office.

"I gave up virtually everything to support what I was doing on the job," she says. "In effect, I married the company."

To her dismay, her last transfer put her back on the staff level, after she had already held a senior post with 45 people reporting to her. "If I had it to do over again, I'd move less," she says.

Now 46 years old, Ms. Kiryluk works as vice president of human resources at Tupperware, a unit of Premark International Inc. The new job allows her to stay in one base, where she says she has "potential for roots."

A DOUBLE-EDGED SWORD

As Ms. Kiryluk and others have discovered, many career-oriented employees without children must contend with a double-edged sword. The commitment and sacrifice that often help them get ahead in their careers may also leave them feeling far behind in other aspects of their lives.

"They see it as dues paying on the fast track," says Jennie Farley, a professor of industrial and labor relations at Cornell University. "Their lives are disrupted more and they pay a high price. We all need a work-life balance."

One solution, employment experts say, is to create company benefits that appeal to a wide range of lifestyles. Programs that don't favor parents are the least likely to breed resentment on the job, says Carol Sladek, a benefits and compensation consultant for Hewitt Associates. If parents are allowed to tailor their work hours to child-care pickup times, then childless workers should be able to leave the office early to attend university classes or look after a sick spouse.

More Equitable Approaches

Some employers are beginning to get the message. In January 1993, Quaker Oats Co. introduced a benefits plan designed in part to be more equitable for childless workers. Fifteen employees of the Chicago-based food company, including three without children, were recruited to develop the plan. It gives childless workers an annual credit of $300 because they generate lower medical insurance costs for the employer. They can use the credit to "buy" up to three extra days of vacation, depending on salary, or extra life insurance or other benefits.

Spiegel Inc., in Downers Grove, Ill., offers flexible hours to everyone. Kelly Daily, a Spiegel human-resources manager with no children, has taken several hours off in the middle of the workday to pick up friends at the airport or to attend her nephew's kindergarten Christmas pageant. She appreciates the latitude her bosses give her. "They know I'm not an eight-to-five worker," says Ms. Daily, who usually stays until 7 p.m. "By being flexible, they know I'm going to give 150% back."

Corning is also doing things differently. For example, the name of its family-support program has been changed to "work/life" and seminars that appeal to people with no children have been added. Single workers are now encouraged to organize their own groups for social outings and community-volunteer projects. Some new courses offer assertiveness training. In one seminar, childless employees practice effective ways to ask for time off for social and recreational needs.

Taking one more step, Corning is also training its managers to offer flexible hours to workers without children and to avoid dumping extra work on them. Says Ms. Werner, the Corning work/life consultant: "That has helped to reduce jealousy between employees."

| "'Ending welfare as we know it' means erasing the value of work that mothers perform in the home, work upon which all of society depends."

WELFARE REFORM THREATENS POOR FAMILIES

Eileen Boris and Gwendolyn Mink

In August 1996, President Bill Clinton signed a welfare reform bill that abolished the federal program Aid to Families with Dependent Children (AFDC) and provided the states with funds to devise their own antipoverty programs. In the following viewpoint, written before the passage of the welfare legislation, Eileen Boris and Gwendolyn Mink criticize a similar proposal by the nation's governors. Boris and Mink contend that welfare reform proposals that include time limits and work requirements neglect the importance of the work women perform in raising their children. These reforms, the authors assert, will push poor single mothers into low-wage jobs outside the home, thereby increasing the economic and social burdens on poor families. Boris, a professor of history at Howard University in Washington, D.C., is the author of Home to Work: Motherhood and the Politics of Industrial Homework in the United States. Mink is a political science professor at the University of California at Santa Cruz and the author of The Wages of Motherhood: Inequality in the Welfare State.

As you read, consider the following questions:

1. According to Boris and Mink, how would the proposal for state-level welfare reform restrict aid to poor families?
2. What is the "founding principle of welfare," according to the authors?

From Eileen Boris and Gwendolyn Mink, "Welfare Reform Doesn't Value Mothers," San Diego Union-Tribune, February 14, 1996. Reprinted by permission of the authors.

President Clinton was right to veto the "Personal Responsibility and Work Opportunity Act of 1995," the Republican majority's plan to shred the federal safety net in the name of "family values." Now the governors have tempered congressional Republican moralism, but have reserved the right to impose moral means tests (like the family cap) on recipients at the state level.

They would further punish single mothers for their poverty through work requirements and time limits. Most important, the governors would repeal Aid to Families with Dependent Children (AFDC), a pillar of the 1935 Social Security Act, and so end the right of poor women and children to economic assistance. Under their plan, welfare would become "an entitlement to states," not people. In his January 1996 budget proposal, the president, too, would replace AFDC's guarantee of aid with a "conditional entitlement" capped by time limits.

State Welfare Reform Has Not Worked

The governors say they can best care for poor people, but it is hard to see how. State-level reforms and budgetary decisions in recent years have worsened poverty in many places; they certainly haven't catapulted poor mothers into jobs at living wages. The governors' proposal restricts Medicaid, food stamps, child protection and child-nutrition services to levels that would put millions in need.

It adds a few billion for child care, but eliminates the requirement that states continue to contribute their own monies for income support, work and child-care programs. The call for additional federal child-care funds is surely welcome, but is only a half-measure. By itself, child care enables, but does not generate, work that pays a family wage.

Welfare reformers are less interested in the quality of jobs and wages than they are in the concept of work. Opposing the "work ethic" to welfare, reformers seek greater moral leverage against poor mothers. It is time to stop "reform" that fights poverty by blaming the poor. Welfare reform must be about work.

Devaluing Mothers' Work

But time limits and work requirements assume that poor, single mothers who care for their children do not work—that they do not expend productive energy, time and effort managing households and nurturing children. This view strikes at the founding principle of welfare: the care of the next generation.

"Ending welfare as we know it" means erasing the value of work that mothers perform in the home, work upon which all of society depends. Welfare "reform" severs the link between the welfare of poor mothers and children and the welfare of us all.

The American public has certainly not rejected the importance of child-raising: Most mothers of young children who work outside the home do so part-time, and many middle-class mothers choose not to earn wages at all. Why do policy-makers insist that poor single mothers—women who already shoulder a double burden in parenting—must work outside the home?

Wasserman ©1995, *Boston Globe*. Distributed by the Los Angeles Times Syndicate.

The racial stereotype of the welfare mother—as baby-machine, unproductive consumer and lazy cheat—obscures the socially imperative work single mothers do in caring for their children.

This image further obscures the conditions under which poor solo parents perform their care-giving work, namely poverty. Welfare politics has long been a terrain of racial politics: The more politicians portray the welfare mother as black, the less worthy the program, the easier to justify its dismantling.

STRUGGLING TO RAISE A FAMILY

The stories of welfare recipients help us understand what's at stake here. A Mississippi woman, Stella Thomas, told a reporter in October 1995: "$144 a month and $397 in stamps isn't enough when you have three kids and you cook every day." Across the country, poor women recount their struggles to raise children—to nurture them, to protect them from urban violence, to supervise homework and generally to ensure survival with dignity under harsh circumstances. Reformers dismiss this work as unproductive, as a drain on the federal budget. This assumes not only that poor mothers are undeserving, but that their children are as well.

Earning less than men, women often find themselves further disadvantaged in the labor market because of their responsibilities as mothers. They take up the slack when schools dismiss sick children, or elderly parents need to visit doctors.

How much more difficult is the combination of outside work and family for single mothers, particularly those whose low wages keep them poor and who can't afford reliable child care or depend on kin or on the fathers of their children? These are the women who have a safety net in AFDC.

LOW-WAGE WORK IS NOT THE ANSWER

Pushing welfare recipients into low-wage jobs is absurd when even childless high school graduates scramble for shifts at fast-food restaurants and the college-educated face pink slips. Forcing these mothers to work outside the home becomes a strategy to discipline low-wage workers, to keep them from demanding better conditions and higher wages or joining unions.

Welfare "reform" emphasizes the work ethic and personal responsibility, condemning poor, single mothers for needing welfare. This ignores the social and economic disadvantages that turn solo motherhood into such travail. Ending poverty as we know it would be a better strategy.

We must raise the minimum wage and link work to social supports that would make it possible for single mothers to perform both their jobs. But that alone isn't enough. We should affirm the work of care-giving, and so recognize its economic and social value.

"[Welfare reform gives] those on welfare what we want for all families in America, the opportunity to succeed at home and at work."

WELFARE REFORM WILL BENEFIT POOR FAMILIES

Bill Clinton

In August 1996, President Bill Clinton signed into law a welfare reform bill designed to enable welfare recipients to work and ultimately eliminate their need for government assistance. Such reform will increase opportunities for poor families, Clinton argues in the following viewpoint. In the past, he maintains, government economic aid to poor families fostered overdependence on welfare, thereby undermining the value of work. Legislation that ensures adequate child care, health care, child-support enforcement, and time limits on welfare will help recipients enter the workforce and eventually pull their families out of poverty, he concludes. This viewpoint is taken from a speech Clinton delivered at a July 1996 news conference in which he defended the legislation that he eventually signed into law in August 1996. Clinton is the forty-second president of the United States.

As you read, consider the following questions:
1. According to Clinton, in what ways has he encouraged work and responsibility during his presidency?
2. Why was the 1995 Republican legislation on welfare unacceptable, in the author's opinion?
3. What welfare reforms have Wisconsin, Oregon, and Missouri proposed, according to Clinton?

Excerpted from Bill Clinton's remarks at a news conference on welfare legislation, as recorded by the Federal News Service, July 31, 1996, and reported in the *New York Times*, August 1, 1996.

G ood afternoon.
When I ran for President in 1992, I pledged to end welfare as we know it. I have worked very hard to do just that.

Today [July 31, 1996] the Congress will vote on legislation that gives us a chance to live up to that promise, to transform a broken system that traps too many people in a cycle of dependence to one that emphasizes work and independence, to give people on welfare a chance to draw a paycheck, not a welfare check. It gives us a better chance to give those on welfare what we want for all families in America, the opportunity to succeed at home and at work.

For those reasons, I will sign it into law. . . .

A HISTORIC OPPORTUNITY

For 15 years I have worked on this problem, as Governor and as the President. I've spent time in welfare offices, I have talked to mothers on welfare who desperately want the chance to work and support their families independently.

A long time ago I concluded that the current welfare system undermines the basic values of work, responsibility and family, trapping generation after generation in dependency and hurting the very people it was designed to help.

Today we have a historic opportunity to make welfare what it was meant to be: a second chance, not a way of life. And even though the bill has serious flaws that are unrelated to welfare reform, I believe we have a duty to seize the opportunity it gives us to end welfare as we know it.

PROMOTING WORK AND RESPONSIBILITY

[Since 1993,] I have done everything in my power as President to promote work and responsibility, working with 41 states to give them 69 welfare-reform experiments. We've also required teen mothers to stay in school, required Federal employees to pay their child support, cracked down on people who owe child support and cross state lines. As a result, child-support collections are up 40 percent to $11 billion, and there are 1.3 million fewer people on welfare today than there were when I took office.

From the outset, however, I have also worked with members of both parties in Congress to achieve a national welfare reform bill that will make work and responsibility the law of the land.

I made my principles for real welfare reform very clear from the beginning. First and foremost, it should be about moving people from welfare to work. It should impose time limits on welfare. It should give people the child care and the health care they need to move from welfare to work without hurting their children. It should crack down on child-support enforcement, and it should protect our children.

This legislation meets these principles. It gives us a chance we haven't had before to break the cycle of dependency that has existed for millions and millions of our fellow citizens, exiling them from the world of work. It gives structure, meaning and dignity to most of our lives.

IMPROVED LEGISLATION

We've come a long way in this debate. It's important to remember that not so very long ago, at the beginning of the 104th Congress, some wanted to put poor children in orphanages and take away all help from mothers simply because they were poor, young and unmarried. [In 1995] the Republican majority in Congress sent me legislation that had its priorities backward: It was soft on work and tough on children. It failed to provide child care and health care. It imposed deep and unacceptable cuts in school lunches, child welfare and help for disabled children.

The bill came to me twice, and I vetoed it twice. The bipartisan legislation before the Congress today is significantly better than the bills I vetoed. Many of the worst elements I objected to are out of it, and many of the improvements I asked for are included.

SOME SINGLE MOMS APPLAUD WELFARE REFORM

Like a lot of people, Lucretia Bailey thinks the nation's welfare system has failed and she is glad that Congress and President Clinton are junking it in favor of a program that emphasizes jobs and limits welfare benefits to five years.

"Welfare makes you lazy. You get accustomed to it," she said. "It kind of makes you not want to achieve more." Welfare reform "makes you really get up and try to help yourself."

What makes Bailey's views particularly interesting is that she is a welfare mother herself, a 23-year-old unmarried mother of one child with another on the way.

Melissa Healy, *Los Angeles Times*, August 3, 1996.

First, the new bill is strong on work. It provides $4 billion more for child care so that mothers can move from welfare to work, and protects their children by maintaining health and safety standards for day care.

These things are very important. You cannot ask somebody on welfare to go to work if they're going to neglect their children in doing it.

It gives states powerful performance incentives to place people in jobs. It requires states to hold up their end of the bargain by maintaining their own spending on welfare. And it gives states the capacity to create jobs by taking money now used for welfare checks and giving it to employers as income subsidies, as an incentive to hire people, or being used to create community service jobs.

Second, this new bill is better for children than the two I vetoed. It keeps the national nutritional safety net intact by eliminating the food stamp cap and the optional block grant. It drops the deep cuts and devastating changes in school lunch, child welfare and help for disabled children. It allows states to use Federal money to provide vouchers to children whose parents can't find work after the time limits expire. And it preserves the national guarantee of health care for poor children, the disabled, pregnant women, the elderly and people on welfare.

Doing Better by Children

Just as important, this bill continues to include the child-support enforcement measures I proposed in 1994, the most sweeping crackdown on deadbeat parents in history.

If every parent paid the child support they should, we could move 800,000 women and children off welfare immediately. With this bill, we say to parents, if you don't pay the child support you owe, we will garnish your wages, take away your driver's license, track you across state lines and, if necessary, make you work off what you owe.

It is a very important advance that could only be achieved in legislation. I did not have the executive authority to do this without a bill.

So I will sign this bill, first and foremost because the current system is broken; second, because Congress has made many of the changes I sought; and third, because even though serious problems remain in the non–welfare-reform provisions of the bill, this is the best chance we will have for a long, long time to complete the work of ending welfare as we know it, by moving people from welfare to work, demanding responsibility, and doing better by children.

However, I want to be very clear. Some parts of this bill still go too far, and I am determined to see that those areas are corrected.

First, I am concerned that although we have made great strides to maintain the national nutritional safety net, this bill still cuts deeper than it should in nutritional assistance, mostly for working families with children. . . .

Second, I am deeply disappointed that the Congressional leadership insisted on attaching to this extraordinarily important bill a provision that will hurt legal immigrants in America, people who work hard for their families, pay taxes, serve in our military. This provision has nothing to do with welfare reform; it is simply a budget-saving measure, and it is not right. . . .

RISING TO THE CHALLENGE

I challenge every state to adopt the reforms that Wisconsin, Oregon, Missouri and other states are proposing to do, to take the money that used to be available for welfare checks and offer it to the private sector as wage subsidies to begin to hire these people, to give them a chance to build their families and build their lives.

All of us have to rise to this challenge and see this reform not as a chance to demonize or demean anyone, but instead as an opportunity to bring everyone fully into the mainstream of American life, to give them a chance to share in the prosperity and the promise that most of our people are enjoying today. And we here in Washington must continue to do everything in our power to reward work and to expand opportunity for all people.

| "Daycare can damage children intellectually, emotionally, and physically."

DAY CARE HARMS CHILDREN

Mary Monica

Parents who place their youngsters in full-time day care are endangering their children's emotional growth, contends Mary Monica in the following viewpoint. According to Monica, studies show that young children must bond with their mothers to develop healthy personalities and self-esteem. If these children are separated from their mothers too often, she maintains, they are likely to display social and psychological problems later in life. To prevent the problems caused by the use of full-time day care, Monica concludes, society should reemphasize traditional family values and full-time motherhood. Mary Monica is the pseudonym for a frequent contributor to Fidelity, a Catholic journal of opinion.

As you read, consider the following questions:

1. According to Monica, how do women who work because of economic necessity feel about their families?
2. How does the author describe a typical infant's experience of full-time day care?
3. What is "masking," according to Monica?

From Mary Monica, "The Real Victims of the Nine-to-Five Dilemma," Fidelity, July/August 1993. Reprinted with permission.

From the late 1960s through the early 1980s, before I began rearing my adopted children, I worked as a full-time secretary for a variety of agencies. These years gave me the opportunity to observe first-hand the policies of different companies towards working mothers and the effects of those policies upon families. One large institution with a staff of over five hundred employees had requested that I research and write an article for their monthly newsletter on flex-time and job-sharing. In compiling data, I interviewed not only women employed by that particular institution, but those who worked in other fields and for different employers. I interviewed clerks, executives, nurses, teachers, housecleaners, factory laborers, therapists, and supervisors. I spoke with mothers who worked less than twenty hours per week, those who worked full time, and those who labored a demanding fifty to seventy hours per week in managerial positions. Some had only a grammar school education; others had earned their Master's degrees. Whatever their occupation or education, however, I soon discovered that they basically fell into two groups: the careerists and those who worked primarily out of economic necessity.

THE CAREERISTS

The careerists clearly expressed that they worked through choice; they spoke scornfully of the very idea of staying at home. Their work was their life, their focal point—their homes and families their sidelines. Their eye on promotions up the career ladder, they attended seminars and workshops, volunteered to take on extra projects, and willingly worked overtime. Several were even pursuing college courses evenings in addition to full-time employment. They worked their daily schedules around their jobs, not around their families' needs. If they had little time with their husbands, if their toddlers were expressing serious behavior problems in daycare, if they only saw their infants for one or two hours per day, well, that was tough.

I remember in particular one thirty-year-old woman who had spent several anxious years and twenty thousand dollars on fertility treatments before she finally had her miracle baby. Yet shortly thereafter, she deposited her beautiful daughter in daycare and returned to her six day a week position. "I wouldn't stay home all day with a kid," she said contemptuously.

LIVING TWO LIVES

The second group, who comprised the majority of those I interviewed, admitted that they were working primarily for economic reasons. Their attitudes towards their families were entirely different. They yearned over their children and felt guilty and devastated in leaving them to be raised by strangers. Because they were not career-primary, they tended to work in more traditional, lower-paying jobs and, unlike the careerists, could not afford to hire housekeepers to assist with the upkeep of their homes. The time of this second group was fragmented four ways: their jobs, their families, their homes, themselves. They found living in the framework of twenty-four hours extremely difficult.

"The cleaning and cooking and laundry that I could have done the eight hours I'm at my job is still waiting for me when I drag in at night," complained one.

"I feel schizophrenic," related a mother of two. "I have to work my darnedest to meet my supervisor's needs, but when I come home totally drained, I still have to meet the very different needs of my family, another full-time job in itself. I feel like I'm living two different lives."

These women were so concerned about not fulfilling their children's needs during their all-day absences, that they spent their evenings and weekends struggling to squeeze out as much "quality time" as possible. To fulfill their responsibilities, they robbed themselves of their own personal time, often not eating or sleeping properly. I became friends with one executive who had four children from age six down. She admitted that she was months behind in her housework, that the only way she could get her laundry and cleaning done at all was to force herself to stay up until three a.m. and work as fast as possible. Her physical health was poor, and she looked exhausted and older than her years, and no wonder. She told me that she had existed on only four hours of sleep per night for the last few years.

Because they were often working against their will, these mothers often resented the time their jobs took away from their families, and some even expressed resentment at their husbands for forcing them to work in the first place. And they felt guilty about the way they treated their children when they finally returned at the end of the day, exhausted.

"My three year old son follows me around, pleading 'Mommy, please play with me.' I'm so wiped out I can barely open a can of soup."

"My toddler hangs on me howling from the moment I arrive home. I'm flying around trying to get the laundry done and supper on the table before my husband gets home, and my son does nothing but scream for attention. Sometimes I have to shut myself in the bathroom just to get away from him."

A registered nurse with school-age children complained, "The minute I step over the threshold my kids descend on me, all having complaints and demands and needs. I'm exhausted from eight hours on my feet, and it's all I can do to keep from shaking my fists and screaming, 'Let me alone! Let me alone till I can unwind!'"

FAMILY NEEDS ARE NOT BEING MET

These women are not ogres. They are simply worn out from having to fulfill two full-time roles simultaneously: homemaker and provider. Most jobs are not the refreshing, fulfilling paradise that feminist literature would have us believe. Few careers are exciting or glamorous. By its very nature, outside employment is demanding and draining—physically, mentally, and emotionally, so that by the time mothers return home, there is little left to give to their families.

Popular psychologist Dr. James Dobson expresses sympathy for the mother "who must arise early each morning, take her children to a child-care center, work eight or nine hours a day at a job, and then try to meet the physical, emotional, and spiritual needs of her youngsters at the end of the day when others are resting. It can't be done! Something will be shortchanged. There is simply not enough energy in the human body to work eighteen hours a day, every day, year in and year out.". . .

THE MOTHER-INFANT BOND

Psychologists know now that an infant begins to learn before birth, and experiments have proven that a newborn can readily recognize and respond to the voice of its mother because he has heard her voice while in the womb. Child psychiatrist Donald Rinsley feels that the mother-infant bond begins to form during the pregnancy itself and is "unique and cannot be fully substituted for by even the most sensitive and caring surrogate mother figure." He expresses that the foundations of the baby's later personality are laid down during this very early bonding period—this first year of life.

In those crucial early weeks, the newborn learns to know and to trust his mother as she comforts him, meets his needs tenderly, communicates with him. Dr. John Bowlby, researcher and child psychiatrist at London's Tavistock Clinic, well-known for his theory of attachment, has written extensively on the importance of early bonding. Unfortunately for many of America's newborns, that deep bond is all too soon snapped. Many corporations only permit a six week childbearing leave before the mother must return to her job. A Christian friend, who provides home-based daycare, recently told me that she had been contacted by a young woman who wanted to know if she would "take a two-week old infant for fifty to sixty hours per week."

THE EFFECTS OF FULL-TIME DAYCARE

What happens to a baby's fragile bond with his mother, his need for stability and regularity, when he is placed in full-time daycare? Let us put ourselves in the child's mind and heart and look at a typical Monday morning. He is awakened out of a sound sleep, whisked from his crib in the predawn hours, hurriedly fed and dressed, deposited in an automobile, and taken to an entirely different environment where he is deprived of the two people he loves most for the majority of his waking hours. He doesn't know where he is, where his parents are, or why they have left him. If he has an older sibling, he is separated from her also, as most daycare centers divide children into age groups. The baby's needs are met, in competition with numerous other howling children, by the faces of strangers, and because daycare staff are usually low-paid, their turnover rate is high, and these faces are frequently changing. A baby has no concept of time, so his parents' absence seems an eternity to him. At the lonely end of this bewildering day, his parents come to claim him—exhausted by their efforts at the office or the factory. When they return home, it is not to relax and enjoy their family. They have dinner to prepare, laundry to catch up, and sundry household tasks to do and can often give the baby only minimal attention before he is fed and put back to bed. From the child's point of view, what an empty and sterile life. And it happens all over again on Tuesday, Wednesday, Thursday, and Friday.

So many books and articles are being written today about the fragile self-esteem of children. What do these daily, lengthy absences of parents communicate to their offspring? That their careers are more important to them than their youngsters are? How does their self-esteem suffer when they frequently hear: "Can't you see I'm busy now?" or "Now what do you want?" or "I said I don't have time!"

A human child has a mind and a soul. He is not a pet that can be conveniently boarded in a kennel, or a tropical fish that can survive in an aquarium with minimal attention. Karl Zinsmeister, author and researcher, writes that, when parents buy daycare, "they are buying much more than a service which permits them to work. They are buying an environment that determines much of what their children—what this society—will become."

The prominent Dr. John Bowlby writes that "the young child's hunger for his mother's presence is as great as his hunger for food" and that "her absence inevitably generates a powerful sense of loss and anger." He feels that the early attachments program a child much like the hard drive of a computer, so that the first impressions are very difficult to change later. He further expresses concern that "by the end of their first year, some children have already given up trying to communicate with their mothers."

The attachment theory predicts that babies are at risk psychologically if separated from their mothers for twenty or more hours per week during their first twelve months of life. Years of experiments by other researchers have proven that fifty percent of daycare babies are insecurely attached to their mothers. Incidentally, this situation applies not only to center-based daycare, but to other forms of non-maternal care as well. Children from affluent homes cared for by nannies still displayed significant insecurity in their attachments. . . .

THE TODDLER YEARS

Even the toddler years are crucial. Psychologists agree that qualities such as sympathy and empathy develop between fifteen and eighteen months of age, and these are dependent on the quality of mothering received during that time frame. The child under age three is still an unformed personality, yet by age four it is estimated that half of his adult character is formed. Parents really have only one opportunity then to shape the traits that their youngsters will carry into every challenge they face in life. Dr. James Dobson explains, "There is a critical period during the first four or five years of a child's life when he can be taught proper attitudes. These early concepts become rather permanent. When the opportunity of those years is missed, however, receptivity usually vanishes, never to return." He points out that "motherhood is a full-time job during the child's first five years. . . . Children need their mother more than they do a newer car or a larger house. . . . Is an eighteen-year-old baby-sitter going to apply the principles of good parenthood . . . Is she going to mold and guide and reinforce those subtle but important attitudes that emerge every day?"

Feminists, of course, would argue, ad nauseam, that "it's not the amount of time, but the quality of time spent with a child that counts." Educator Raymond Moore has a succinct answer for that: "For those mothers who suggest that they give 'quality time' in lieu of quantity of time, we feel constrained to ask if they or their husbands may do that at the office."

Separation from Parents Harms Children

Liberated ladies point out that after working an eight-hour shift, mothers still have sixteen hours left in the day to nurture their children. Their mathematics are far off; the period of separation is far greater. While eight hours may be spent actually working, most companies have an unpaid lunch break, bringing the actual time spent at the work place to nine hours. Add to that any overtime, plus travel time to and from work, and the hours of absence can increase to ten or eleven. I interviewed one dual-earner couple who admitted they spent a total of three hours per day simply commuting to their factory jobs in the city. The wife explained that she dropped her two small sons off at the baby-sitter's house at 6 a.m. and usually did not pick them up again until 6:30 p.m. She also complained that the children were sassy and disobedient (a common complaint, I noticed, of mothers who worked long hours), yet I could scarcely blame these small boys for refusing to take direction from a mother who was absent virtually all their waking hours. Almost all of their needs were being met by a baby-sitter; they did little at home on weekdays, save sleep. . . .

Day Care Health Risks

There is a large and growing body of evidence that day care is a breeding ground for infectious diseases. The mere act of separating an infant from his mother may suppress the immune system and make the child more vulnerable to disease. Putting a number of young children together increases exposure to disease. Compared to children cared for at home in a six-month period, children in day-care homes are 25 percent more likely to contract infections, while those in day-care centers get nearly 50 percent more infections and are nearly three times as likely to need hospitalization. Medical costs for children in day care are close to 100 percent to 200 percent higher.

J. Craig Peery, *The Family in America*, February 1991.

Gene Armeto, who operated four large daycare centers in New Jersey, explains, "This is the reason why confusion reigns. The child truly does not know or understand what is going on and to whom he should turn for security and trust. Simultaneously, the child may continually receive mixed messages—one set of values, rules, and functions at home and, probably, another set in the daycare facility."

Indeed, studies done throughout the 1970s and 1980s have

proven that youngsters in full-time daycare, especially those who have enrolled as infants, displayed more negative social behaviors: verbal and physical aggression, excessive physical activity, reduced toleration for frustration and stress, and more antagonism towards adults.

The University of North Carolina did a study of children in kindergarten and the first grade and discovered that the youngsters who had been enrolled in center-based daycare during their infancy were more inclined to kick and hit, as well as threaten and swear at their peers, than those who were raised by full-time mothers.

In addition to warping the developing child's character, extensive daycare can stress the child emotionally. According to Karl Zinsmeister, "One widespread source of childhood stress is the increasing separation of children from their parents at young ages. . . . Many doctors and child psychologists report sharp increases in the number of children exhibiting psychosomatic and stress-related illnesses. Childhood admissions to psychiatric wards are up. . . . The teenage suicide rate has tripled in the last thirty years. . . . A very worrisome pile of research is now accumulating which suggests that, when the very young go into extensive nonparental care, many—possibly most of them—will suffer emotional and intellectual harm."

Working Mothers Face Stress

Few employers realize the enormous stresses placed upon employed mothers. Feminists told corporations that women could perform as well as men, that sex had nothing to do with that performance, and the corporations took them at their word. I actually heard supervisors warning my former co-workers: "Don't bring your personal problems to work with you," or "don't let your family troubles interfere with your work life." How can a mother avoid bringing her troubles to work with her if she has been up all night caring for a sick toddler or walking the floor with a colic-stricken infant? One cannot schedule such events conveniently on weekends. The very nature of a job demands that a woman perform well at it, or risk demotion or dismissal. Some mothers have actually been terminated because they took off too much sick time to care for ailing children.

A few years ago, I was employed by the personnel office of a large agency. This agency was proud of the fact that they employed more females than males, and many of the former were mothers with young children. Concerned with the amount of family sick leave the staff was using, the agency developed a sick leave procedure that really amounted to a disciplinary measure. Any usage of leave that was not approved by the supervisor one day in advance was labelled an "unscheduled absence." If an employee had four unscheduled absences within a three month period she was called on the carpet for what was ominously called a "counselling session," and her record was duly marked. There was little flexibility for illness or emergency. If a mother stayed home for three consecutive days to care for a child with measles, each of those three days was considered a separate "unscheduled absence." Understandably, the mothers were very upset at being "counselled" for nursing their sick children.

THE PROBLEM OF "MASKING"

When women are put under pressures such as these, there will be abuses, and unfortunately the innocent youngsters are the ones to pay the price. When a parent cannot afford to take off one more sick day, or if they fear being "counselled" for using too much time, they will dose the child with Tylenol to temporarily hide the fever and other symptoms and drop the child off at daycare without mentioning to the staff that the little one is ill. This practice has grown so common that daycare centers have even coined a term for it: it is called "masking." By the time the Tylenol has worn off, and the baby is spiking a high fever again, the parents have managed to put in part of their work shift.

The frequency of masking has made daycare centers breeding places for infectious disease. The immune systems of babies are naturally immunodeficient, and their chances of contracting illnesses are tremendously increased when daily exposed to large groups of other youngsters. A study in the *Pediatrics* publication stated: "Parents of children in daycare can expect the infant to be sick nine to ten times per year, and a preschooler to be sick six to seven times per year with respiratory infections." The January 1990 *American Journal of Epidemiology* reported that youngsters in daycare centers have 3.5 times the risk of diarrhea, cramps, upset stomachs, and other such intestinal illnesses than those remaining home with mothers. The November 9, 1989, issue of the *New England Journal of Medicine* reported that twenty-five to sixty percent of children in daycare acquire cytomegalovirus (CMV) which can cause birth defects in pregnant women. This not only puts female daycare staff at risk, but the mothers of these daycare youngsters as well. Physicians have even created a name for this syndrome: it is called "daycaritis." Mothers are being warned by the Public Health Department in some areas to have their offspring immunized against diseases linked with daycare before even enrolling them in these centers.

A CHILD'S NIGHTMARE

Thus, daycare can damage children intellectually, emotionally, and physically. Yet the liberal, profeminist media have kept many of these vital facts from the public. Child care is considered analogous to women's rights. Yet as grim as this damage to children is, there is another aspect to daycare even more sinister: the numerous cases of neglect, abuse, and even sexual molestation in licensed daycare facilities. From 1983 to 1985, for example, a study made by the University of New Hampshire divulged that in the licensed daycare facilities alone, there were 1,639 cases of confirmed sexual abuse. In one of our southern states, dozens of little ones in a particular daycare center were diagnosed with gonorrhea of the mouth. Children have been forced into disgusting sex acts with each other, with adults, and even perversions with animals. Some have been used as actors in the production of pornography. Thomas Case wrote an excellent feature in the January 1990 issue of *Fidelity* entitled "Satanism Rising: It's 1990; Do You Know Where Your Children Are?" describing ritualized/satanic abuse of youngsters in daycare centers. To children trapped in such situations while their parents pursue their careers, the entire adult world has become a nightmare. . . .

The real victims of the nine to five dilemma, then, are the helpless children who have no voice to protest the injustices committed against them. It is the children whose needs are being put on the back burner, who are being deprived, neglected, or even aborted in the name of careerism. Let us, as laity, ask our bishops and priests to speak forcefully for a return to traditional family values.

> "Research has indicated many
> benefits for children in high-quality
> child care arrangements."

DAY CARE CAN BENEFIT CHILDREN

Kristin Droege

Some researchers and social scientists believe that the use of full-time day care damages the mother-child relationship and therefore hampers a child's social and psychological development. In the following viewpoint, Kristin Droege argues that high-quality day care can actually advance children's development. Research has shown that peer group interaction in high-quality day care centers encourages healthy emotional and intellectual growth in children, Droege contends. She concludes that the government should inform working parents about child care options and subsidize high-quality day care. Droege is a research associate at the Milken Family Foundation in Santa Monica, California.

As you read, consider the following questions:

1. When was day care first used in the United States, according to Droege?
2. According to the author, what is attachment theory?
3. Why is licensed day care better than the use of family relatives for child care, in Droege's opinion?

From Kristin Droege, "Child Care: An Educational Perspective," *Jobs & Capital*, Winter 1995. Reprinted by permission of the publisher, The Milken Institute for Job & Capital Formation.

The term child care is used to refer to any form of care for children that is not provided by parents. Child care centers, the most familiar form, exist in many churches, synagogues, and community centers, and have since the mid-1980s appeared both in the parents' workplaces (in the form of corporate-sponsored programs) and in the for-profit sector. Family day-care homes, in which a woman provides child care in her own home, are also a very popular style of child care. Other arrangements include in-home nannies and au pairs; independent preschool and nursery school programs; early childhood programs established through universities and private or parochial schools; and having children stay with a friend, neighbor, or relative for regular and consistent periods of time throughout the week.

A Brief History of Child Care

Child care is not new to American culture. The first day nurseries were established in the mid-1800s when the industrial revolution brought women out of the homes and into the factories. During the Great Depression, public funds were first applied toward child care as an attempt to provide work for unemployed teachers, nurses, cooks, and janitors. Then came World War II. With women working in the factories, child care boomed. By 1945 over 1.5 million children attended child care. When the war ended, so did the boom. In the mid-sixties, with the women's movement, preschool programs and early childhood education began growing in popularity again. At this time, early childhood also became the focus of increased attention from researchers in the fields of psychology and education. Today, early childhood education and child care are almost indistinguishable. Almost every care arrangement for children under the age of six claims to provide the child with an environment and activities that will assist the child's growth physically, intellectually, socially, and emotionally. Parents and educators now commonly expect that child care is meant to serve the needs of working parents while simultaneously benefiting the development of the child.

What do we actually know about children's needs throughout the preschool years and the impact of full-time child care arrangements on their development? Research has analyzed several areas of development in relation to children's child care experiences. The earliest research focused on children's attachment relationships, examining the possibility that separation from the mother, especially during infancy, could damage the mother-child relationship believed to be so influential on later social development and competency. Research later shifted to include more direct study of the impact of child care on social development. Social development throughout childhood plays a crucial role in preparing the child to function successfully in society. The mother-child attachment relationship and later social skills developed with adults and peers predict the individual's ability to maintain friendships, working relationships, intimate relationships, and parental relationships in later adult life.

The Early Mother-Child Relationship

Since 1985, attachment theory has gained enormous popularity in the field of developmental psychology. Based on the work of John Bowlby, attachment theory asserts that children, predominantly through their interactions and experiences with their mother during the first year of life, develop an internal working model of their own value as a human being and the role of "others" in their life. Simply stated, if a child receives sensitive and responsive caregiving in the first year of life, attachment theory predicts that the child will develop a working model of himself as worthy of love. He also develops a view of "others" as generally trustworthy and good. A sensitive and responsive caregiver consistently and appropriately responds to the child's social bids, or requests, and initiates interactions that are geared to the child's capacities, intentions, moods, goals, and developmental level. The child's internal working model, or view of the role and importance of self and others, would result in a secure attachment relationship with the mother.

On the other hand, a child whose mother is insensitive to her needs, unresponsive to her bids, or, in the extreme case, abusive or neglectful, is expected to develop an insecure attachment relationship with her mother. The insecure relationship is the result of an internal working model of the child as unworthy of love and of "others" as insensitive or untrustworthy. It is believed that the internal working model that is developed in infancy serves as a basis for the child's approach to social interactions and relationships throughout life.

While attachment theory resembles psychoanalytic theory to some extent in placing such great importance on early maternal relationships, it is distinguished by an important body of empirical research that supports Bowlby's ideas. Beginning with the work of Frank Ainsworth, psychologists have developed techniques to operationalize Bowlby's principles and classify children according to the security of their attachment relationship with their mother. Intensive examination of mother/child interactions has linked specific mothering behaviors to the child's attachment classification. Later work based on attachment classification examined the child's success in peer groups and friendship formation. Research has confirmed that children whose mothers are sensitive and responsive during infancy are more likely to develop secure attachment relationships with their mother and later are more successful with peers in school and other social interactions than are children with insecure attachment relationships.

THE EFFECTS OF CHILD CARE

With such strong evidence of the importance of mother/child interactions in early childhood, it is no surprise that attachment theory posed serious concerns about the social development of children who attended child care during infancy. If sensitive and responsive caregiving by the mother is vital to the formation of a secure attachment, long separations from the mother could threaten the attachment relationship. Early research depicted a grim view of children's attachments with their mothers after the children were placed in full-time care, arguing that children who spent extensive time in child care during infancy were more likely to have insecure attachments with their mothers and exhibited heightened aggressiveness and noncompliance in preschool.

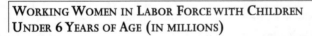

WORKING WOMEN IN LABOR FORCE WITH CHILDREN UNDER 6 YEARS OF AGE (IN MILLIONS)

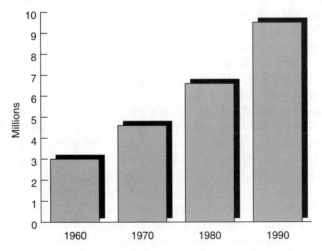

Kristin Droege, *Jobs and Capital*, Winter 1995.

As the body of research on the subject grew, however, it became clear that the effects of child care were not so clear-cut. Two further waves of research resulted. While the first wave of researchers was still arguing over whether or not child care was good for children's development, the second wave began examining the differences in the care provided to children who had secure versus insecure attachment relationships. How does the kind of child care provided influence child development and, specifically, attachment? Researchers found easily identifiable markers of care that produced positive versus negative developmental outcomes in children. These markers came to be identified as indicators of high-quality child care. Children who spent time in high-quality child care were just as likely to have secure attachment relationships with their mothers as children who stayed at home. It was also discovered that children who had insecure attachment relationships with their mothers, but who attended high-quality child care, were capable of forming secure attachment relationships with their child care providers. A sensitive and responsive child care provider may compensate for a mother/child relationship that is insecure. The picture was, therefore, not so grim when the quality of the child care arrangement was considered.

CHILDREN'S SOCIAL DEVELOPMENT

Researchers have continued to explore the impact on children's social development of high-quality child care and greater exposure to a large peer group during infancy and the preschool years. Not only do we know that children who receive high-quality care appear more socially competent with peers than those in low-quality care, the research indicates that high-quality child care may, in fact, provide benefits to children that they do not receive in the typical home setting. The social importance of the early childhood peer group was elaborated by J. Rubenstein and Carollee Howes, who suggested that children in child care with peers use their peers as a source of social support to assist with the separation from mother. Further, their work suggested that play with peers who have comparable cognitive and motor skills facilitates common interests and pleasures and allows previously acquired skills to be elaborated and elevated to more complex levels. For instance, a toddler may be able to roll the ball down the slide, but with a peer the game encourages a 'give and take' situation with turns, in which one child rolls the ball down and the other pushes it back up. This expands the child's skills and abilities in both the social and cognitive realm. While the same interaction might take place with an adult a few times, it truly takes a peer to enjoy enacting this procedure 20 or 30 times in a row for several days on end until it is no longer novel and exciting.

THE BENEFITS OF HIGH-QUALITY CARE

Further research has indicated many benefits for children in high-quality child care arrangements. Children with child care experience appear less timid and fearful, more outgoing, help-ful, and cooperative with unfamiliar peers than children with-out child care experience. Children who have experience with a stable group of peers demonstrate social play skills that are more complex and reciprocal than those whose peer group has been unstable due to frequent changes in child care arrangements. Children who have experienced a stable peer group are more likely to function successfully in the social relationships they will experience in later childhood and adulthood, such as those encountered in school, work, and family settings.

Researchers have created a framework for conceptualizing characteristics of child care programs that predict positive chil-dren's outcomes. Markers of quality care are broken down into structural and process quality. Structural quality includes charac-teristics such as adult/child ratio, group size, salary and benefits, and education and training of the staff. Process quality includes the provision of developmentally appropriate activities for chil-dren, and sensitive and nurturing caregiving. The National Child Care Staffing Study, a study of 227 child care centers across five major metropolitan American cities, indicated that structural and process quality are related. Children receive more appropriate and sensitive caregiving in centers with lower ratios, smaller group sizes, and well-educated and trained teachers. . . .

WHO IS USING CHILD CARE TODAY?

It is not startling to hear that the number of women in the labor force has been steadily rising since 1975. Yet the impact of this sociological shift on the field of child care has been dramatic. Over 9 million women with children under the age of six were working in 1990. In 1991, there were 11.1 million children under the age of six with both parents (or their sole parent, in single-parent homes) working. That number was expected to increase to 14.6 million by 1995. In contrast, the number of spaces for children in regulated child care facilities, while in-creasing, has not matched the increase in demand. A study by Mathematica Policy Research in 1990 found that 80,000 child care centers existed, serving between 4 and 5.1 million children. While the number of centers tripled between 1976 and 1990, the number of children using child care centers had quadrupled, meaning that spaces were even harder to find. One-quarter of all child care centers were filled to capacity, and the majority of centers had utilization rates of 93 percent or more.

Seeing the high demand for child care spaces, the for-profit industry has entered the child care field. Both nationwide chains and independent "mom and pop" for-profit centers are available in many communities. In comparing child care center quality by the sponsorship of the center (for-profit vs. nonprofit), the NCCSS (National Child Care Staffing Study) found that for-profit centers, both chain and independent, paid lower wages to teachers and directors, had higher staff turnover rates, and provided fewer benefits than nonprofit or church-based centers. Teachers in for-profit centers had lower levels of education and experience in the field than did teachers in nonprofit or church-based centers. Overall, for-profit care received lower ratings than nonprofit or church-based centers with regard to the adult work environment provided, the characteristics of the teachers employed, and the child development environment created; each of these factors had been found to be related to the developmental outcomes of the children.

THE PROBLEM OF LOW-QUALITY CARE

One of the most common options parents choose for the care of their young children is the use of relatives. Approximately 20 percent of all working mothers place their young child in the care of relatives, either in their own home or in the home of a relative. However, *The Study of Children in Family Child Care and Relative Care* found that 69 percent of all of the relative care examined proved to be inadequate care. Relative care received lower quality ratings than licensed family day-care homes. While many parents feel it is safest and most convenient to leave their child with a family member, licensed family day-care providers were more likely to plan activities for the children, and had more training in the field than did the relatives.

This is not to say that the nonprofit market has not responded at all to the increased demand for child care spaces. More child care centers and family day-care homes exist today than ever before and they continue to open at high rates. So some might say that the real problems are short-term and that the market will respond to provide the necessary number of care facilities. However, there are a few problems with that scenario, and they revolve around the issues of quality that I have discussed.

The first problem is one of information. Some families who can afford the price of high-quality care choose lower-quality care because they lack information about the benefits of high-quality care, what high-quality care looks like, and how to find it. A distressing obstacle to high-quality child care is the centers' ability to disguise the quality of their care. Many parents visit and inspect the child care center that they intend to use for their child. The information that is conveyed by a 20-minute visual inspection of a child care center can, however, be misleading and deceptive. It is much cheaper for the center to invest in brightly colored decor, posters of children playing, and brochures that tout a rich and varied curriculum than it is to raise teacher wages, increase opportunities for teacher education and training, and lower adult/child ratios and group sizes. These substantive issues are much more difficult or uncomfortable for a parent to discover, and usually decisions are made based on the superficial appearance of the program. Thus, parents are not likely to receive substantive information about the quality of care their child will receive at any particular center.

One solution is to educate parents about the importance of a high-quality child development program, what high quality means, and how to identify it. Government investment in the creation and dissemination of information about early childhood education would be a public service that could benefit the larger community. Better information could educate parents about the importance of such issues as turnover rates and educational backgrounds of caregivers, and assist parents in asking the questions necessary to elicit such information.

INVESTMENT IN CHILD CARE

The next problem is the loss of social benefits. Society has an interest in children being prepared to enter school. Yet many parents choose not to use high-quality care because of considerations other than the quality of the child development program. When parents make the decision to enroll their child in child care they must weigh many factors into the equation. Most parents probably consider the first priority to be a program that keeps their child safe, healthy, and happy. But simultaneously they take into account the convenience of the center's location, the hours that the center remains open, its policy for sick children and late pick-ups, and, most important, the fees that the center charges. When parents choose a center they often trade off their standards concerning the quality of its child development program in exchange for their logistical needs or their budget.

Thus, if people buy only the child care they are willing or able to pay for, they tend to buy lower-quality care than is optimal for the larger society. An additional investment, however, which could provide a higher-quality child development program, extended hours, or a broader sick-child care program, would benefit the larger community as well as the individual family and child. For the community, for example, this investment could yield children attending the local public schools who are more socially skilled, cognitively advanced, with more advanced communication skills, and thus more likely to succeed academically.

Since this additional investment in child care yields benefits to the larger community, it merits our attention to find additional sources of funding. Although some oppose government investment in child care, they have in fact always contributed to the expense of caring for the young children in our country through the lost tax revenues of women who worked in their homes raising their children. Government investment in quality child care programs can yield social benefits to children, families, and the broader community.

Moreover, (some) parents may value child care quality less highly than their children would if the children were able to make such spending decisions. Accordingly, government can be viewed as a player substituting for the invisible care-quality preferences of children; subsidies for child care thus may be appropriate.

PERIODICAL BIBLIOGRAPHY

The following articles have been selected to supplement the diverse views presented in this chapter. Addresses are provided for periodicals not indexed in the *Readers' Guide to Periodical Literature*, the *Alternative Press Index*, the *Social Sciences Index*, or the *Index to Legal Periodicals and Books*.

Joshua Abramowitz	"The Democrats' Welfare Trap," *National Review*, April 4, 1994.
Diane Eyer	"Is Mother-Infant Bonding a Myth? *Glamour*, July 1993.
Jaclyn Fierma	"Are Companies Less Family-Friendly?" *Fortune*, March 21, 1994.
David A. Hamburg	"The American Family Transformed," *Society*, January/February 1993.
Diane Harris	"Big Business Takes on Child Care," *Working Woman*, June 1993.
Dirk Johnson	"Family Struggles to Make Do After Fall from Middle Class," *New York Times*, March 11, 1994.
Charisse Jones	"Family Struggles on Brink of Comfort," *New York Times*, February 18, 1995.
Mickey Kaus	"Tough Enough: A Promising Start on Welfare Reform," *New Republic*, April 25, 1994.
Peter T. Killborn	"More Women Take Low-Wage Jobs Just So Their Families Can Get By," *New York Times*, March 13, 1994.
Julia Lawlor	"The Bottom Line on Work-Family Programs," *Working Woman*, July/August 1996.
Karen Levine	"Is Today's Workplace Really Family-Friendly?" *Parents*, August 1993.
Social Justice	Entire issue on women and welfare reform, Spring 1994.
Jodeen Wink	"Listen: True News of a Welfare Mother," *Humanist*, September/October 1995.

CHAPTER 4

WHICH ADOPTION POLICIES DESERVE SUPPORT?

CHAPTER PREFACE

In April 1995, the Warburtons, a Chicago couple, were required to give their adopted son back to his birth parents. The child, referred to as "Baby Richard," had been adopted as an infant in 1991. Shortly after the adoption, however, Otakar Kirchner, the child's biological father, sued for custody of the boy. Kirchner argued that his parental rights had been denied because he had not been informed of his child's existence until after the adoption. After years of litigation, the Illinois Supreme Court ruled in favor of Kirchner. Many among the public and the legal community were surprised by the court's decision to allow a four-year-old to be taken from the only home he had known.

This spotlight on the conflict between the rights of birth parents and the rights of adoptive parents led to calls across the country for more consistent adoption policies. In 1994, the National Conference of Commissioners on Uniform State Laws (NCCUSL) proposed a Uniform Adoption Act (UAA). This act, which has been introduced into some state legislatures, calls for several reforms: allowing biological fathers to make a parental claim no more than thirty days after the adoption process has begun, encouraging birth parents to become more aware of legal and emotional issues before giving a child up for adoption, and requiring adoption records to be closed for ninety-nine years. According to journalist Susan Chira, supporters "say the proposed law would require courts to consider what is best for children and close crucial legal loopholes."

Opponents of the Uniform Adoption Act, however, argue that it is a conservative measure that would favor the rights of adoptive parents and limit those of adopted children and birth parents. For example, many adoption-related groups, including Concerned United Birthparents and Adoptees in Search, contend that the proposed law would deny adult adoptees the right to know about their birth circumstances, medical history, and genetic heritage. Other adoption groups fear that the UAA would reverse the trend toward open adoptions, which they claim allow children to form healthy relationships with both their biological and adoptive parents.

Recent years have witnessed many controversies over adoption policies. The authors in the following chapter probe some of these ongoing debates.

> "There are many childless couples . . . who have the emotional and financial stability to make good families, and there are millions of babies killed who could have gone to such couples."

ADOPTION SHOULD BE PROMOTED AS AN ALTERNATIVE TO ABORTION

Maria McFadden

Adoption should be advocated as an alternative to abortion for women experiencing an unwanted pregnancy, argues Maria Mc-Fadden in the following viewpoint. Although the media have publicized negative reports about adoption, McFadden contends, many childless couples would make excellent parents for un-wanted children. She maintains that giving up a child for adoption is difficult but more ethical than choosing to abort a fetus. McFadden is the executive editor of Human Life Review, a quarterly conservative journal that focuses on abortion and related issues.

As you read, consider the following questions:

1. Why might a woman view her abortion as a "good deed," according to McFadden?
2. In the author's opinion, why have pro-choice activists attacked adoption?
3. How does P.D. James's novel The Children of Men reflect on the problem of contemporary selfishness, in McFadden's opinion?

Abridged from Maria McFadden, "Rapping Abortion," Human Life Review, Summer 1993. Reprinted by permission.

Imagine a modern-day scenario. Two women somewhere in America get pregnant—unexpectedly. Neither wants her child. One decides to abort the fetus and donate its flesh and organs to medical research; by her human sacrifice, she thinks she might be able to save a life, perhaps help a Parkinson's patient. The other thinks at first about adoption: Wouldn't someone want her child, considering all she has heard about couples and infertility? Couldn't she make someone happy and give her child life?

But then she thinks more and more about the arguments against it: How can she bear not knowing where her child is, if he or she will be cared for; she has heard many stories lately about adopted children being abused or growing up "dysfunctional" and haunted by their status. She has seen that made-for-TV movie (based on a true story) about a teenage mother who was forced to give up her baby—when she went to find him 20 years later, she found he had died at age 10, beaten to death by his adoptive mother. And there are so many older children who need to be adopted, and . . . well, once she sees her child it will be too painful to give it up anyway. So she has an abortion.

IS KILLING A NOBLE CHOICE?

If we assume that these two women were influenced by the mores of the liberal media, the first would probably say (whatever she might actually feel) that she not only exercised her constitutional right, but she did a good deed for another. In a recent Redbook poll on fetal tissue research and its effect on abortion, one woman said: "A woman's decision would certainly be swayed if she thought she could justify it by telling herself she was doing mankind some good by her choice." The second woman might also say that she did a noble thing, by "saving" her child from an uncertain future, and she did what was right for herself, too.

The common denominator, of course, would be that both babies were killed, in the name of "higher" principles. And yet not so long ago the decision to kill either child would have been abhorrent, and the decision to "give away" both for adoption the noble, life- and love-giving answer.

ADOPTION UNDER ATTACK

It should not surprise us that, with the attacks on traditional morality of the past thirty years, adoption—a traditional answer to unwanted pregnancies—would come under attack as well. Since abortion has steadily become a matter of a woman exercising her right not to be inconvenienced by a pregnancy, asking a woman to go through the inconvenience anyway but not keep the child doesn't make Feminist sense. One might have thought that if people were less ashamed about unmarried sex and unwanted pregnancies, there might at least be more support for unwed mothers who want to donate a child to someone else. Instead, adoption has become the latest issue "outed" by the media. Like alcoholism, sexual abuse, and dysfunctional families, adoption now has its bitter victims—birth mothers who were "forced," adopted children who have suffered abuse, adoptees and birth mothers who go through their lives never feeling whole (although I have yet to read of an adoptee who would rather have been aborted).

This "outing" of adoption, like the campaign for "abortion reform" in pre–Roe v. Wade days, has become a regular feature in the liberal (read pro-abortion) media, and the campaign has been highly effective. In addition to the smear campaign in the newspapers and magazines (plus books with titles like Shedding Light on the Dark Side of Adoption and Death by Adoption), TV movies and "perversion-of-the-week" talk shows—those great teachers of social morality—have been steadily barraging Americans with negative stories about adoption.

The reason is, at least partially, that "pro-choicers," since the Webster decision, have made adoption a particular target. [In the 1989 case of Webster v. Reproductive Health Services, the Supreme Court barred the use of public facilities for abortion and limited access to late-term abortions.] Webster made them realize pro-lifers could still win some battles in the abortion war, and pro-lifers were touting adoption as an abortion alternative, so the attacks had to be stepped up on pro-lifers and any cause they embraced. Adoption is of course a choice, but the deathly logic of the abortion-rights lobby compels the "choicers" to scream (pardon the words) bloody murder whenever an alternative to abortion is presented. Every decision to bring an "unwanted" baby to term is a political and ideological loss for the "choicers," as it is for the monetary interests of the abortion industry. Furthermore, those who refuse to admit the life present in a fetus will naturally balk at that fetus being looked at as a potential adopted child.

ADOPTION CAN WORK

Sad to say, though, even some on the anti-abortion side have at times joined the anti-adoption crusade, perhaps unwittingly, by publicizing stories of adopted children and their mothers reuniting after a life of "never feeling whole." These heart-tugging stories are in favor of life, or there wouldn't be a child to reunite with, but they imply that adoption doesn't ever work, whereas there *are* many happy adopted children and adoptive parents. Less than five per cent of adoptees search for their birthparents, and it would be interesting to ask the other 95 per cent if they felt reasonably "whole," but that wouldn't make for good *Oprah*.

Asay. Reprinted by permission of Chuck Asay and Creators Syndicate.

Adoption is not a perfect solution; it is difficult for everyone involved. So is life. But the fact remains that there are many childless couples who are broken-hearted over their inability to have children, and who have the emotional and financial stability to make good families, and there are millions of babies killed who could have gone to such couples. Tragically, there are also thousands of children without parents, not because no one wants them, but because they have been rendered unadoptable by a maze of laws, policies and prejudices which favor biological parents' rights and discourage trans-racial and trans-national adoptions. You won't hear this from the media—you will hear that white couples don't want to adopt black children, that people don't want handicapped kids, that no one wants older children. We are all meant to feel guilty about bringing another child into an adoption pool who will go ahead of these "rejects." These negative ideas are so prevalent that their validity is hardly investigated by the press. . . .

THE SIGNIFICANCE OF FAMILY

There is no experience that can compare with having a family and—even though we seem to have forgotten it—that is what we humans are here to do: make families, clans, communities. We have a huge glut in this country of pregnancies, and an awful dearth of newborns; we have a glut of unwanted older children whose souls are being strangled by the neglect and abuse perpetuated by monstrous, bias-twisted laws. And we have all sorts of desperate women running to sperm banks or IVF [in vitro fertilization] clinics. The child that one woman callously aborts would have made some desperate women ecstatic—but "reproductive choice" dictates that no one ask for such a sacrifice and exchange.

In P.D. James' powerful novel *The Children of Men*, the human race of the future is dying out—suddenly, in one brief time period, all men and women are completely sterile. The last generation to be born is treated like gods, and as there are no babies, dolls and pets are treated with grotesque care—christenings of cats, elaborate pantomimes with dolls. Sex, being then completely divorced from the possibility of procreation, has lost its appeal to most survivors.

This frightening futuristic fantasy world takes the sins and selfishness of our age to their logical extreme, and the consequences are ghastly. How many childless people today spend their heart's capacity on animals alone, when there are so many children that might be loved? (How many people who applaud the pulling apart of live fetuses for use in fetal-tissue transplants protest medical experiments on animals, which are meant to help us cure human diseases?) Yes, children are riskier, more involving—you will never be the same once you open your heart to your child, but perhaps that brings us to the basic problem of our age: Are we as humans living for pleasure and the least amount of aggravation, or is anything worthwhile in life going to involve pain and sacrifice? Families certainly involve the latter, but, as with adoption, the beauty of families exists not in spite of but because of the scars.

Finally, as *The New Yorker* says [in a May 10, 1993, commentary that is sympathetic to adoption proponents], there is a "power that the heart has over blood." That's what adoption is all about, and it's also about giving, sacrificing, and realizing that good parents aren't only those who can conceive naturally—good parents are people who will love, nurture and provide for children. It's the simplest truth—but can we hear it amid the shouts of the "pro-choicers" who bitterly oppose a choice that saves a child?

| "Promoting adoption instead of abortion sounds life-affirming, but it's actually physically dangerous, cruel and punitive."

ADOPTION SHOULD NOT BE PROMOTED AS AN ALTERNATIVE TO ABORTION

Katha Pollitt

In the following viewpoint, Katha Pollitt contends that policy-makers should not always advocate adoption as an alternative to abortion. Pollitt maintains that there are not enough adoptive parents available for all unwanted children. Moreover, she argues, it is wrong to pressure women into taking on the difficult process of pregnancy and childbirth for the sake of potential adoptive parents. Women should instead feel free to choose abortion with no repercussions, she concludes. Pollitt is an associate editor for the Nation, a progressive journal of opinion.

As you read, consider the following question:

1. In Pollitt's opinion, what is wrong with the claim that more than one million Americans each year wish to adopt?
2. How many Chinese baby girls did Americans adopt in 1995, according to the author?
3. Why do so few girls and women choose to give up children for adoption, in Pollitt's opinion?

Katha Pollitt, "Subject to Debate: Adoption Fantasy." Reprinted with permission from the July 8, 1996, issue of the Nation magazine.

Bill Clinton loves it. Bob Dole, too. Newt Gingrich thinks it's so terrific he wanted to mass-produce it through the Personal Responsibility Act. Hillary Clinton told *Time* she dreamed of trying it herself. As the "family values"/teen-sex/abortion debate winds on with no end in sight, adoption is being touted as a rare area of consensus: the way to discourage "illegitimacy" while providing poor children with stable homes, the peace pipe in the abortion wars. Whatever may be the difficulties and conflicts of actual people involved in the adoption triangle, at the political level, it's all win-win: adoption and apple pie.

Whenever I question the facile promotion of adoption as a solution to the problem du jour I get angry letters from adoptive parents. So I want to be clear: Of *course* adoption can be a wonderful thing; of *course* the ties between adoptive parents and children are as profound as those between biological ones. But can't one both rejoice in the happiness adoption can bring to individuals *and* ask hard questions about the social functions it is being asked to fill? I can't be the only person who has noticed that the same Administration that supports the family cap—the denial of a modest benefit increase to women who conceive an additional child while on welfare—is about to bestow on all but the richest families a $5,000 tax credit to defray the costs of adoption. Thus, the New Jersey baby who is deemed unworthy of $64 a month, or $768 a year, in government support if he stays in his family of origin immediately becomes six times more valuable once he joins a supposedly better-ordered household. Maybe unwed mothers should trade kids.

Adoption Is Not a Cure-All

In 1995, mass adoption was supposed to rescue innocent babies from the effects of defunding their guilty teenage mothers—a bizarre brainstorm of social scientist Charles Murray that has fortunately faded for now. In 1996, adoption was back in a more accustomed role, as an "alternative" to abortion—a notion long supported by abortion-rights opponents from Ralph Reed to Christopher Hitchens, and recently picked up by some pro-choicers too. The wrong women insisting on their right to have children, the right women refusing to—it's hard to avoid the conclusion that as public policy, adoption is being pushed as a way of avoiding hard questions about class and sex. After all, if poverty is the problem, we could enable mothers and children to live decently, as is done throughout Western Europe. If teenage pregnancy is the problem, we could insist on contraception, sex education and health care—the approach that has also worked very well in Western Europe, where teens are about as sexually active as they are in this country, but where rates of teen pregnancy range from half of ours (England and Wales) to one-tenth (the Netherlands).

ABORTION IS NOT A SELFISH CHOICE

There are many different reasons why women get abortions. And they are all valid. No woman should feel guilty about terminating an unwanted pregnancy. And no woman should buy the crap that having an abortion is "selfish."

The birth of a child can be a source of great joy to a woman. But it can be a nightmare for a woman who *for whatever reason* does not want to have a child at a particular time or under particular circumstances. In such cases *forcing* a woman to continue a pregnancy is extremely cruel and sadistic. It will affect her entire life, and no woman's life should be twisted in such a way.

Revolutionary Worker, January 15, 1995.

How much sense does adoption make as a large-scale alternative to abortion? Journalists constantly cite the National Council for Adoption's claim that 1-2 million Americans wish to adopt —which would make between twenty and forty potential adopters for every one of the 50,000 or so non-kin adoptions formalized in a typical year. But what is this estimate based on? According to the National Council for Adoption, it's a rough extrapolation from figures on infertility, and includes anyone who makes any gesture in the direction of adoption—even a phone call—which means they are counting most of my women friends, some of the men and, who knows, maybe Hillary Clinton too. The number of serious, viable candidates is bound to be much smaller: For all the publicity surrounding their tragic circumstances, in 1995 Americans adopted only 2,193 Chinese baby girls. Even if there were no other objections, the adoption and abortion numbers are too incommensurate for the former to be a real "alternative" to the latter.

TERMINATING A PREGNANCY IS NOT SELFISH

But of course, there are other objections. There are good reasons why only 3 percent of white girls and 1 percent of black girls— and an even tinier percentage of adult women—choose adoption. Maybe more would do so if adoption were more fluid and open—a kind of open-ended "guardianship" arrangement—but that would surely discourage potential adoptive parents. The glory days of white-baby relinquishment in the 1950s and 1960s depended on coercion—the illegality of abortion, the sexual double standard and the stigma of unwed motherhood, enforced by family, neighbors, school, social work, medicine, church, law. Those girls gave up their babies because they had no choice—that's why we are now hearing from so many sad and furious 50-year-old birth mothers. Do we really want to create a new generation of them by applying the guilt and pressure tactics that a behavior change of such magnitude would require?

Right now, pregnant girls and women are free to make an adoption plan, and for some it may indeed be the right choice. But why persuade more to—unless one espouses the anti-choice philosophy that even the fertilized egg has a right to be born, and that terminating a pregnancy is "selfish"? I'm not belittling the longings of would-be adoptive parents, but theirs is not a problem a teenager should be asked to solve. Pregnancy and childbirth are immense events, physically, emotionally, socially, with lifelong effects; it isn't selfish to say no to them.

Promoting adoption instead of abortion sounds life-affirming, but it's actually physically dangerous, cruel and punitive. That's why the political and media figures now supporting it wouldn't dream of urging it on their own daughters. Can you imagine the Clintons putting [their daughter] Chelsea through such an ordeal? Hillary Clinton is entitled to her adoption fantasy, but maybe she ought to think a little more about the girls who are already here. They have a right to put themselves first.

"What parentless children need are not 'white,' 'black,' 'yellow,' 'brown,' or 'red' parents, but loving parents."

SOCIETY SHOULD FACILITATE TRANSRACIAL ADOPTIONS

Randall Kennedy

Adoption policies that favor placing children with parents of their own race are misguided, argues Randall Kennedy in the following viewpoint. Minority children—particularly black children—constitute a large percentage of youngsters in need of adoption, Kennedy maintains, and they often must wait years before being placed in permanent homes. Requiring these children to wait until prospective parents of their own race can adopt them cruelly extends the amount of time they spend without a permanent family, Kennedy contends. Moreover, he asserts, same-race adoption policies are based on racial stereotypes and faulty generalizations. Kennedy is a professor at Harvard Law School.

As you read, consider the following questions:

1. What is the Multiethnic Placement Act, according to the author?
2. According to Kennedy, how does the policy of racial matching deter some prospective parents from adopting minority children?
3. What is wrong with the belief that black adults generally make better parents for black children, in Kennedy's opinion?

From Randall Kennedy, "Orphans of Separatism." Reprinted with permission from the *American Prospect*, Spring 1994. Copyright 1994, The American Prospect, PO Box 383080, Cambridge, MA 02138.

No issue more highlights feelings of ambivalence over the proper place of racial distinctions in American life than the delicate matter of transracial adoptions. Opponents of such adoptions insist that allowing white adults to raise black children is at worst tantamount to cultural genocide and at best a naive experiment doomed to failure. In most states, custom reflects and reinforces these beliefs; public policy, formally or informally, discourages cross-racial adoptions or foster placements, to the point where thousands of children are denied placement in loving homes.

THE MULTIETHNIC PLACEMENT ACT

Now one of the Senate's leading liberals is compounding the damage with a well-intentioned but badly misguided bill titled the Multiethnic Placement Act. Senator Howard Metzenbaum of Ohio sees his bill as a deft compromise. On the one hand, the bill prohibits state agencies or agencies that receive funds from the federal government from completely barring or unduly delaying transracial child placements, either for adoptions or foster care. This aspect of the bill has provoked the opposition of those who strongly favor racial matching, the policy that seeks to place children of a given race with foster parents or adoptive parents of the same race. On the other hand, the bill evinces a preference for racial matching by explicitly stating that race may be taken into account in making child placement determinations and by prohibiting only *undue* delays caused by efforts at racial matching (thereby implicitly authorizing some delay). This preference stems from Metzenbaum's own belief that "every child who is eligible for adoption has the right to be adopted by parents of the same race," and that "teaching a child self love and to embrace their racial and cultural heritage is more easily accomplished when parents and children are of the same race or ethnic group." [The Multiethnic Placement Act was signed into law in October 1994.]

Metzenbaum thus embraces *moderate* racial matching. While he does not favor barring transracial child placements altogether, he views such arrangements as distinctly less desirable than racially matched child placements. Many intelligent, caring, thoughtful people of good will agree with Senator Metzenbaum. His legislation is supported by Marian Wright Edelman's Children's Defense Fund and is echoed by an editorial in the *New York Times*, which declared that while total prohibition of transracial adoptions is unwise, "Clearly, matching adoptive parents with children of the same race is a good idea."

These good people are wrong. To understand why and the stakes involved in their error, one must confront [a number of] overlapping social disasters.

A SOCIAL CATASTROPHE

The first is the fact that increasingly large numbers of children bereft of functioning parents are flooding social welfare agencies. Agencies are charged with maintaining these young refugees from destroyed families and either placing them in the temporary care of foster parents or the permanent care of adoptive parents. According to Metzenbaum, the number of such children has exploded from 276,000 in 1986 to 450,000 in 1992—a vivid and concrete manifestation of what happens when poverty, crime, and substance abuse tear families apart.

Like most social catastrophes in the United States, this one weighs most heavily upon racial minority communities: the percentage of minority children in need of foster care or adoptive homes is far greater than their percentage of the population. In Massachusetts, approximately 5 percent of the population is black, yet black children constitute nearly half of the children in need of foster care or adoptive homes. In New York City, 75 percent of the nearly 18,000 children awaiting adoption are black. Nationwide, there are about 100,000 children eligible for adoption; 40 percent are black. While two years and eight months is the median length of time that children in general wait to be adopted, the wait for black children is often twice that long.

Conceiving of the deprivations suffered by children without parents is both easy and difficult. It is easy because some of the things that we expect parents to do are so obviously important. We expect parents to protect the interests of their children in a singular fashion, to show a degree of loyalty that cannot be bought, to demonstrate a mysterious allegiance deeper than professional duty. It is difficult because of the enormity of even attempting to calibrate the manifold, subtle, perhaps even unknowable losses borne by parentless children. There is one thing, however, about which we can be sure: it is a tragic condition indeed for a child to be condemned to the limbo of parentlessness, to suffer the loneliness of having no one to call "mother" or "father," to be exposed to the anxiety of having no family that is permanently and intimately one's own.

RACIAL MATCHING IS A DISASTER

A second social disaster compounds the first. It is the disaster of racial matching itself. Racial-matching policies can vary in intensity, from absolute prohibitions against transracial child placements to temporary preferences for same-race placements. Examples of the former are state laws in the segregationist Jim Crow South that forbade adoption across the race line and, more recently, the position of the National Association of Black Social Workers, which categorically opposes transracial adoptions involving black children and white parents. Examples of the latter include the customary practices of many social workers around the country and statutes like the ones in California, Minnesota, and Arkansas which require that social workers spend a given amount of time—90 days in California—seeking a same-race adoption for children before they are made available to prospective adoptive parents of a different race.

Bok. Reprinted by permission of Chip Bok and Creators Syndicate.

Racial matching is a disastrous social policy both in how it affects children and in what it signals about our current attitudes regarding racial distinctions. In terms of immediate consequences, strong forms of racial matching block some parentless children from access to adults who would otherwise be deemed suitable as parents except that they are disqualified on the grounds that they are of the "wrong" race. In some jurisdictions, the relevant decision-makers simply refuse to permit child placements across the color line. In others, authorities will permit foster care across racial lines but then remove the child if they move to deepen the relationship from mere temporary foster care to permanent adoption. In still other jurisdictions, social welfare agencies delay placing children with adoptive parents of the "wrong" race until efforts are undertaken to place the child with parents of the "right" race. Delay of any length is, of course, a cost in and of itself. While three months might seem like a negligible delay from the perspective of adults, such delays are lengthy indeed from the perspective of infants. Moreover, for many adults, children become less attractive as adoptees as they age. What seems at first like mere delay may obliterate the chance of some youngsters for adoption at all; prospective adoptive parents willing to adopt a child of six months may not be willing to adopt the same child at one year.

THE CONSEQUENCES OF RACIAL MATCHING

Furthermore, given that racial matching mirrors and reinforces the belief that same-race child placements are better and therefore preferable to transracial arrangements, some adults seeking to become foster or adoptive parents are likely to steer clear of transracial parenting. Some adults who would be willing to raise a child regardless of racial differences find themselves unwilling to do so in the face of social pressures that stigmatize transracial adoption as anything from second-best to cultural genocide. What this means in practice is that racial matching narrows the pool of prospective parents, which in turn either delays or prevents the transmission of children in need of parents to adults able and willing to serve as parents. How much misery this adds to our pained country is difficult to calibrate. That racial matching adds a substantial amount of misery, however, is inescapable.

The other level on which racial matching is disastrous has to do with its diffuse, long-term moral and political consequences. Racial matching reinforces racialism. It strengthens the baleful notion that race is destiny. It buttresses the notion that people of different racial backgrounds really are different in some moral, unbridgeable, permanent sense. It affirms the notion that race should be a cage to which people are assigned at birth and from which people should not be allowed to wander. It belies the belief that love and understanding are boundless and instead instructs us that our affections are and should be bounded by the color line regardless of our efforts. . . .

There is no rationale sufficiently compelling to justify preferring same-race child placements over transracial placements. One asserted reason for favoring same-race placements (at least in terms of black children) is that African-American parents can, on average, better equip African-American children with what they will need to know in order to survive and prosper in a society that remains, in significant degree, a pigmentocracy. This rationale is doubly faulty.

First, it rests upon a racial generalization, a racial stereotype, regarding the relative abilities of white and black adults in terms of raising African-American children. Typically (and the exception does not apply here), our legal system rightly prohibits authorities from making decisions on the basis of racial generalizations, even if the generalizations are accurate. Our legal system demands that people be given individualized consideration to reflect and effectuate our desire to accord to each person respect as a unique and special individual. Thus, if an employer used whiteness as a criteria to prefer white candidates for a job on the grounds that, on average, white people have more access to education than black people, the employer would be in violation of an array of state and federal laws—even if the generalization used by the employer is accurate. We demand as a society a more exacting process, one more attentive to the surprising possibilities of individuals than the settled patterns of racial groups. Thus, even if one believes that, on average, black adults are better able than white adults to raise black children effectively, it would still be problematic to disadvantage white adults, on the basis of their race, in the selection process.

No Evidence Supports Same-Race Adoption

Second, there is no evidence that black foster or adoptive parents, on average, do better than white foster or adoptive parents in raising black children. The empirical basis for this claim is suspect; there are no serious, controlled, systematic studies that support it. Nor is this claim self-evidently persuasive. Those who confidently assert this claim rely on the hunch, accepted by many, that black adults, as victims of racial oppression, will generally know more than others about how best to instruct black youngsters on overcoming racial bias. A counter-hunch, however, with just as much plausibility, is that white adults, as insiders to the dominant racial group in America, will know more than racial minorities about the inner world of whites and how best to maneuver with and around them in order to advance one's interests in a white-dominated society.

Who Are the Best Parents for Black Children?

To substantiate the claim that black adults will on average be better than white adults in terms of raising black children, one must stipulate a baseline conception of what constitutes correct parenting for a black child—otherwise, one will have no basis for judging who is doing better than whom. Metzenbaum and other moderate proponents of racial matching imply that white foster or adoptive parents will be, on average, less capable of instilling within a black child an appropriate sense of self-worth and an appropriate racial identity. There exists, however, no consensus on how best to raise a black child (or, for that matter, any other sort of child) or on what constitutes a proper sense of self worth or on what constitutes an appropriate racial identity or on how one would go about measuring any of these things. Is an appropriate sense of blackness evidenced by celebrating Kwanza, listening to rap, and seeking admission to Morehouse College? What about celebrating Christmas, listening to Mahalia Jackson, and seeking admission to Harvard? And what about believing in atheism, listening to Mozart, and seeking admission to Bard? Are any of these traits more or less appropriately black? And who should do the grading on what constitutes racial appropriateness? Louis Farrakhan? Jesse Jackson? Clarence Thomas?

Some moderate proponents of racial matching contend that, on average, white adults seeking foster or adoptive children will be less able than similarly situated black adults to tell these children how best to meet the racial impediments they will surely face. But what is the best advice to give? Blacks do not agree. Nor do whites. Again the key point is that there exists no consensus on how best to raise a black child or any other child.

RACIAL SCREENING IS WRONG

In light of this lack of consensus, the tenuousness of our information regarding the relationship of racial status to social knowledge, the ever-growing complexity of our multicultural society, and our well-taken aversion to official racial distinctions in the absence of clear, strong justifications for them, our government should reject any scheme that engages expressly in racial steering on the basis of a hunch that certain people—because of their race, color or national origin—will know better how to raise a child than other people of a different race, color, or national origin. If officials are satisfied that adults seeking foster or adoptive children are safe, sober folk, they should have to pass no racial screening. What parentless children need are not "white," "black," "yellow," "brown," or "red" parents but loving parents.

| "Transracially adopted children . . . are oftentimes viewed as aliens in the white community and traitors in the black community."

TRANSRACIAL ADOPTIONS CAN BE COUNTERPRODUCTIVE

Felicia Law

In the following viewpoint, Felicia Law argues that transracially adopted children of color often have difficulties developing healthy identities because they do not grow up within their own culture and among members of their own race. Research conducted by supporters of transracial adoption has promoted the belief that race is not important in adoption decisions, she points out. However, she contends, other studies have revealed that many transracial adoptees experience social and psychological problems because they do not have a strong sense of racial identity or self-esteem. Law wrote this viewpoint when she was a Ronald E. McNair scholar at the University of California at Berkeley.

As you read, consider the following questions:

1. What indicators reveal low self-esteem among transracial adoptees, according to Law's survey?
2. According to the author, why does the National Association of Black Social Workers disapprove of transracial adoption?
3. What problems have some postadolescent blacks experienced because of transracial adoption, according to Law?

Excerpted from Felicia Law, "Transracial Adoptions: A Case of Colorblind Love or Cultural Genocide?" *Berkeley McNair Journal*, Summer 1993. Reprinted with permission.

Since the 1960s there has been a push towards integration in various aspects of American life, ranging from schooling and employment policy to adoption practices. Our oftentimes idealistic American culture preaches that race is no longer significant so we no longer need to place labels on people due to their racial background. In essence, American society is on a fast track to becoming colorblind. This notion of a "colorblind" society has created a serious dilemma. While many feel this is the only way for America to be truly integrated, others feel this type of philosophy is extremely problematic.

A prime example of this clashing of viewpoints is displayed in transracial adoption practices. The operational definition of a transracial adoption is the adoption of a child of a different race or ethnicity from their adoptive parents. However, the number of adoptive parents are overwhelmingly white and the children are overwhelmingly of color.

ADOPTION OR CULTURAL GENOCIDE?

There are two specific viewpoints around this issue. The advocates of transracial adoptions tend to argue that love has no color and that all agency-held children deserve a chance to have a family, whether the parents are black, white, Asian, or otherwise. The opponents argue that while children do need families, transracial adoptions are a form of cultural genocide. They believe that a parent of a different race is not as equipped to educate a child about issues concerning self-esteem and racial identity.

My preliminary survey examines the following issues: Are self-esteem and racial identity mutually exclusive? Can white parents rear a child of color to be proud of their [own] ethnic background and rich heritage? If not, what are the implications for cultural genocide?

The 512 families surveyed were taken from an earlier study conducted by William Feigelman and Arnold Silverman. The parents were asked to fill out questionnaires that focused on their child-rearing experiences. This viewpoint will examine . . . quantitative data collected from white [families] with [adopted] Korean [children]. Due to the fact that there has not been an abundance of research done on white-Korean adoptions, I will present the literature on white-black adoptions as a basis for comparison. Although Koreans and African Americans have different histories, many parallels are evident in regard to transracial adoptions. . . .

Although researchers use various tests to measure self-esteem, this author believes it is still extremely difficult to measure a person's self-esteem using scales. [An] operational definition of self-esteem is belief in oneself in terms of identifying with a racial group as an individual and in a group setting. To evaluate the child's self-esteem, questions were posed concerning any behavioral or emotional difficulties, drug matters, problems in school, and problems with the law. There were virtually no hard numbers that would indicate maladjustment or low self-esteem for transracially adopted Asian children. 72% have never had a drug or alcohol problem; 73% never had problems with the law; and 83% had never been expelled or suspended from school. The sample's mean g.p.a. [grade point average] was a 2.6; the majority of the adoptees were in college or had obtained a degree; 35% were gainfully employed; and their Global Assessment Score, measuring their social and psychosocial life adjustment, was 78 (scale ranges from 1 to 100), indicating an above average adjustment. Although minimal symptoms of emotional difficulties may be present, problems only sometimes get out of hand.

There were only two quantitative indicators of low self-esteem. First of all, 59% [of the adoptees] had seen a doctor or counselor for emotional problems. Also, when the children were between the ages of 13–18, 32% indicated that transracial adoptions had caused their self-esteem to be somewhat negative. Although parents did express a concern about supporting their child's racial identity, most only took two steps to ensure that this would happen. One concludes that this, too, contributed to these low levels of self-esteem.

RACIAL IDENTITY DEVELOPMENT

When asked how often the child expressed a feeling of racial pride, 35% responded "never or hardly ever"; 49% stated "sometimes or often"; and 5% responded "all the time." The same type of positive distribution was found for questions about shame, with 65% never or hardly ever feeling embarrassed about their race; 73% never or hardly ever making negative comments about their race; and 60% often or occasionally expressing an interest in learning more about their ethnic backgrounds. These children get along equally well with Asians and whites, with only 2% getting along poorly with whites.

On the other hand, 45% responded that they do feel some discomfort over physical appearance. A related question was posed in which respondents were asked what caused their discomfort (e.g., skin, speech, hair, etc.). Respondents expressed the most discomfort due to facial features (28%) and [they] also expressed general concern about being different from others in their communities (25%). A few adoptees took active steps to change this feeling of being different. For instance, one young Korean girl stated that she did not like her Asian eyes for she knew they made her different. As a result, she explored plastic surgery options to change her eyes. Although she did not go through with the surgery, these types of responses demonstrate the obstacles these children encounter when their self-image and identity is not reinforced or affirmed. In addition, between the ages of 13 through 18, 26% of the respondents indicated that the transracial adoptions had a somewhat negative impact on their racial or ethnic pride. . . .

WHAT DOES PAST RESEARCH TELL US?

The majority of the research conducted on transracial adoptions examines the development of racial identity and self-esteem, parental attitudes, and psychosocial adjustment. Just as the general population appears to be divided on this issue, so are many social scientists and child welfare agencies.

In terms of opposition, the National Association of Black Social Workers (NABSW) in 1972 was the first group to go public with their disapproval of transracial adoptions. As outlined in the 1979 article "Racial and Cultural Issues in Adoption" by C.E. Jones and J.F. Else, the NABSW opposed transracial adoptions because of "fears of cultural genocide on the one hand, and concern for the child's identity on the other." They, like other opponents, felt white homes would not teach African American children to "1) develop positive identities; 2) learn the survival skills necessary in a racist society; and 3) develop the cultural and linguistic attributes crucial to functioning effectively in the black community." Other researchers share similar ideologies. L. Chestang states that African American children must be taught to function in both black and white society. This dual personality, a survival skill, can only be taught by African Americans. Black children reared by responsible black parents will have learned the tools necessary to cope with America's racism. In addition, a black child raised in a black community has the option to retreat to his or her community for solace when pressures mount. Transracially adopted children, however, are oftentimes viewed as aliens in the white community and traitors in the black community. This child will have virtually no identity and will become an outcast in both communities. This has serious implications for identity formation. Not only do these children suffer psychologically, but many go to serious extremes in hopes of fitting in. These extremes range from attempts to changing their appearance, like the Korean girl mentioned earlier, or an all-out denial or withdrawal from their racial group, adding fuel to the cultural genocide argument. In situations like this where a constant identity struggle exists, the children suffer from low self-esteem and experience profound adjustment problems.

THE OUTCOMES OF TRANSRACIAL ADOPTIONS

Research findings on outcomes of transracial adoptions suggest that most of the children become relatively healthy, emotionally stable young adults. But some other findings suggest that the formation of a positive and unambiguous racial identity may be particularly problematic for minority children in white families growing up in a race-conscious society.

To adopt a race-neutral stance and deny the significance of the child's race in family-placement decisions is to negate a very significant part of the child's background. Transracially adopted children must know more than just their racial background; they must learn to cope with racism, to be in the minority most of the time and to adjust to having very different phenotypic as well as genotypic characteristics from their families.

Ruth G. McRoy, *Insight*, June 5, 1995.

Despite these concerns, most of the literature is overwhelmingly in support of transracial adoption. These advocates state that all a child really needs is a loving family and a "human identity." A racial identity is secondary. Researchers like F. Wardle contend that this idea of "cultural genocide" is preposterous, for it places the preservation of a group above the basic needs of individuals. The preservation of African American culture is placed at a higher value than that of providing a child with an inalienable right—a family. The concern should be for the child first. Many studies have documented the positive adjustment of transracial adoptees. However, problems, like self-esteem and racial identity conflicts, may arise as the adoptees reach some later stage of development. . . .

IDENTITY AND SELF-ESTEEM

Identity, as defined by Erik Erikson, a pioneer in identity studies, is the "creation of a sense of sameness, a unity of personality . . . individual and communal." In essence, a child's ethnic identity becomes an extension of the child's individual identity. The main concern here is the issue of whether or not transracially adopted children have higher or lower self-esteem than intra-racially adopted children.

Advocates state and research supports the idea that the most pertinent factor in a child's psychological development is his or her ability to have a strong human identity. Thus, race is considered secondary. [Researchers] R.J. Simon and H. Altstein describe transracial adoptions as a world where the philosophy of pluralism and multiculturalism prevails. They conclude that transracial adoptions offer children the chance to be socialized into two different worlds, resulting in a positive self-image. They continue to argue that this unique racial experience provides children of color with a greater sense of security and an appreciation of two distinct cultures. As a result, transracially adopted children learn that blacks and whites are capable of living in one compatible and egalitarian society. Other studies confirm that transracial adoptees wonderfully adjust to their respective families. Such studies have led many researchers to argue that transracial adoptions do not affect the child negatively and that these adoptees are equally adjusted and confident about themselves if not more than intraracially adopted children. Furthermore, the studies claim that black children are comfortable with their blackness and are as comfortable in their interaction with whites. Even though children who are adopted at a later age do have more adjustment difficulties, some research shows transracially adopted children have equal levels of self-esteem and do exhibit racial pride. However, proponents of this view feel that self-esteem does not influence racial identity.

RACE IS A SERIOUS ISSUE

This evidence, though well documented, is problematic for those on the other end of this argument. While research in favor of transracial adoptions attempts to separate self-esteem and racial identity, other research shows how the two are intertwined. Much of this research is qualitative but this connection sheds a different light on the advocates' research. It shows that if a black child or any child of color does not identify with or has negative perceptions of their race, this child, in essence, suffers from low self-esteem. Children raised by white parents are often-times taught to see the world through colorblind lenses. We are part of the human race first and foremost.

According to a 1984 study by Ruth McRoy, many [trans-racially adopted] blacks have been told by other blacks that they act "different." They do not act or talk like other blacks and their behavior is more in line with whites. Transracial adoptees are not prepared when someone questions their "blackness" or ethnic identity because they have been ill-prepared by their parents. Racial differences are not discussed, and when racial problems occur, many white parents make it into a problem that all people experience, not just blacks or other ethnic minorities. This philosophy of racial dissonance, downplaying a child's racial background, has a serious effect on self-esteem and pride. J. Ladner states:

> It may be that parents do not consider color to be important, but such a blind attitude toward the role of group difference in this society is unwise. Failure to [discuss racism] will obviously leave the child unprepared to understand and deal with the first time he or she is called a "nigger" or some other racial slur.

Although many truly believe that race is not an issue in child-rearing, it is evident that race is a serious issue that must be discussed. To deny that inequities due to race are prevalent in American society and to tell a child that they are human first and ethnic second leaves the child open to a gamut of emotional problems. These children live in a hostile environment where people of color are victimized daily.

Transracial Adoptees Face Painful Adjustments

In general, the [surveyed] adoptees do have a strong identification with their racial group and good levels of self-esteem. However, the fact that 45% stated that they did feel some discomfort over their physical appearance and 57% have seen a doctor or counselor because of emotional problems should not be forgotten. Needless to say, if a child considers an operation on their eyes because it sets them apart from their peers, there is definitely a problem. When a child is told that race does not matter and all they need is a "human identity," there is definitely a problem. . . .

Research shows that adjustment problems can be extremely painful. In a telling article in the *Wall Street Journal*, post-adolescent blacks tell of their experiences as transracially adopted children. Nathan Hutton says he began switching between sounding "black or white": "I don't feel I'm being me around black people . . . they aren't like us . . . I resigned myself to not being black . . . I'm not going to act something I don't want to be . . . who is to say I have to be black? . . . it's so trivial." According to the article, Nathan craved acceptance. He yearned to fit in so much that he allowed people to make jokes at his own expense, and at age five stood on a window sill while pounding his chest shouting "I'm a nigger! I'm a nigger!" Another black male in the article said growing up in a white family hurt his development because self-love was not taught. He wanted to belong so badly that he rubbed his kinky hair on a carpet in hopes of getting the straight, silky look that his white peers had. In the 1984 McRoy study, adoptees were asked about their perception of the black family and what it would be like to live in one. The adoptees said "we'd be discriminated against, we wouldn't be as rich, we'd be teased, we'd be whipped more, and we couldn't go out in public without people staring, and our friends wouldn't ask why we're black."

TRANSRACIAL ADOPTION MUST BE SCRUTINIZED

Given these telling personal experiences, it is clear why many believe transracial adoption leads to cultural genocide. It is evident that these children dislike their appearance, have stereotypical images of blacks, believe that they are better than blacks, and will do anything to change their appearance so as not to be associated with blacks. The formation of human identity is as important as ethnic identity. When black, Indian, Asian, Latino or Chicano children view themselves as white, there clearly is a problem. These are not well-adjusted children with regard to the questions of identity. According to Ladner, this denial manifests itself "just as often in the child's self-image or lack of self-esteem." Although the author believes that all sides concerned do want children of color to have permanent families, future research must ask if this practice is truly healthy for a child of color growing up in a society where race is not declining in significance but increasing.

"There is generally a deep-seated need on the part of the adoptees to know their biological origins, regardless of the quality of family life in their adopted families."

STATES SHOULD OPEN ADOPTION RECORDS

Ruth B. Ward

In most states, birth and adoption records are sealed and can only be opened by court order. In the following viewpoint, Ruth B. Ward argues that these state laws should be reformed to allow adult adoptees access to their original birth and adoption records. Ward maintains that knowledge of one's biological background is an intrinsic need; therefore, she contends, the right of adoptees to know their genetic heritage should be considered a basic human right. Ward is a freelance writer living in Maryland.

As you read, consider the following question:

1. According to Ward, why are an increasing number of adoptees seeking out their birth records?
2. What are the most common arguments that attorneys use when petitioning to open adoptee birth records, according to the author?
3. Why do many courts deny an adoptee's petition to open his or her birth records, according to Ward?

Excerpted from Ruth B. Ward, ". . . By Any Civilized Standard," Humanist, September/ October 1995. Reprinted by permission of the author.

Whether they were adopted in infancy or in early childhood, most adoptees never knew their biological parents or, in muted memory, experience them as vague, unidentifiable figures. There comes that "age," however, when many adoptees' thoughts and energies begin to focus on a search to know about and, in many cases, to meet with their natural parents.

These kinds of missions are undertaken by adults more often today than was the case in past generations. Increased numbers of adoptees in the population and more effective advocacy groups lobbying legislatures for changes in adoption statutes, as well as support and search groups, account for the increase.

To Find One's Roots

There is a psychology upon which these frustrating, often relentless searches are conducted. A psychological portrait of the emotional orientations of many adoptees and their natural parents was drawn by a psychologist who had seen, in a professional relationship, an adoptee-appellant who was petitioning a state court of appeals for access to adoption records.

In a general observation for the court, the psychologist asserted:

> There is generally a deep-seated need on the part of the adoptees to know their biological origins, regardless of the quality of family life in their adopted families. This desire does not necessarily manifest itself in a wish to form a relationship with their family of origin but a need to know something of their biological origins. Conversely, there is often a parallel desire on the part of the natural parents to know something of the lives of their biological children. Preventing this information from being available, when requested by either party, only encourages doubt and uncertainty based on the part of the children and guilt on the part of the natural parents.

Legislatures and courts are increasingly being petitioned to address this emotionally charged issue.

Open Versus Sealed Records

The different organizations represented in the adoption network nationwide are defined by their position on "open" versus "sealed" records when it comes to court proceedings seeking access to original birth and adoption records. For some, "open" means that the adoption and original birth records can be accessed with no legal obstacles; the access can be had simply upon request of the adoptee and other relevant parties to the adoption. Other groups insist that a more limited "openness" is desirable and support limiting information to medical histories and to mutually consenting voluntary registries for identification purposes. And other groups urge maintenance of the status quo in most states, where adoption and original birth records are "sealed" and require court petitions to gain access.

These statutes represent a legislative judgment that confidentiality promotes the integrity of the adoption process and bears rational relationship to state objectives—namely, a legal acknowledgement and establishment in law that confidentiality performs a vital role in balancing the interests of all parties. The prohibition against seeing the records applies equally to the adoptee, adopting parties, natural parents, and any curious party who seeks to look at the record. These statutory provisions for sealed records are a commendable attempt to consider the interests of all parties in the adoption proceeding. However, weighing and balancing these interests is a very different act to affect with justice for all.

Adoption statutes in many states provide that a judge with jurisdiction has the authority, upon showing of "good cause," to unseal the records. This proviso requires the adoptee to file application with the court for "good cause" as to why these records ought to be opened. Most of the states with statutes sealing records include the "good cause" clause, but it is not a uniform clause in all states' adoption legislation.

Court petitions brought by adoptees are adjudicated on a case-by-case basis, and the judges, in most of these cases, exercise narrow latitude in interpreting the law when rendering decisions.

FUNDAMENTAL RIGHTS

Trial court arguments for access to birth records for adoptee petitioners are based most often upon the position that the state statutes sealing original birth and adoption records of the adoptees infringe upon a fundamental right to their own identity and that this infringement, serving no compelling state interest, violates the fundamental right to an identity; that these statutes create a suspect classification, thereby violating the equal-protection clause of the U.S. Constitution; that adulthood is of itself "good cause"; and that statutes denying adult adoptees access to this information are unconstitutional.

In cases relying upon these arguments, judges have generally refused to unseal records. But an eloquent advocacy of this position was delivered in the case of *Petitioner-Appellant v. The People of the State of Illinois*, when the petitioner's attorney argued:

The fact that we are dealing here with a fundamental right is illustrated by the questions we all have about ourselves. What are the physical characteristics to which my children may be genetically prone? What is my ancestral nationality or religious persuasion? What sufferings and endurances are in my roots? What achievements or feats can I point to with ancestral pride? Can anyone seriously deny that one's identity is an inalienable and fundamental right? Thus, the right to know one's individually created identity must be considered a fundamental right. For those persons that are adopted, however, the only way that this fundamental right can be meaningful is to include within it one's liberty to know the identity of his genetic parents. In my opinion, this inclusion is demanded within the quintessential meaning of the fundamental right to know one's individually created identity. . . .

This issue of "fundamental rights" is a powerful and persuasive argument and has become a bulwark position in establishing appeal strategy in many of these cases, despite its lack of success in courts to date.

The Right to Privacy

The U.S. Supreme Court has held that the right of privacy is a fundamental right, while judgments denying access to birth and adoption records affirm that the right to know one's identity, asserted by the adoptees in these cases, is not a "fundamental right." Indeed, one side of the argument asserting that it is not a "fundamental right" is the fact that these cases concern the most intimate areas of personal and marital privacy.

Adult Adoptees

Mind you, [adoptees searching for their birth parents] are not children living out fantasies about nicer parents or teens in the throes of rebellion. The overwhelming majority are adults between the ages of 26 and 35—people of an age to know there is much more to parenting than conception and birth (many of them are parents themselves), adult children who have made peace with their adoptive parents' human failures and entered into a mature relationship with them. Most are supported—even urged to search—by their adoptive parents.

Carol Luebering, St. Anthony Messenger, April 1993.

In the opinion of many judges, the statutes denying open access to records are based upon valid rationales, among which are that adoptees often develop countervailing interests in direct conflict with other parties, particularly the biological parents, and that the privacy interests of the biological parents remain, in many cases, very strong. On the issue of privacy rights, the courts must evaluate the needs of the adoptee with those of other parties concerned.

Court verdicts of denial, in most cases, have been based upon the notion that a statutory assurance of confidentiality encourages the surrender of children for adoption and serves to protect the natural parents from public disclosure of a traumatic emotional event and from the possible intrusion into their lives by a child given up years before. It also serves to protect the adoptive parents from interference from the natural parents in raising the child and facilitates the formation of an integrated, autonomous family unit. *This latter opinion does not address the fact that, at the time the adoptees petition the court, they, too, are adults.* . . .

BY ANY CIVILIZED STANDARD

There are no guilty persons in adoption record cases, no defendants or plaintiffs; there are only petitioners pleading their despair.

How high a premium should the law exact from the innocent to protect from intrusion the sacrosanctity of that altar of privacy rights? Conversely, why must a past mistake, long buried, be compounded by its resurrection years later to satisfy the demands of an unknown or vaguely remembered son or daughter? Can that lady with the blindfold, emblematic of integrity and promise, truly deliver equal justice for all parties in these cases? Each of us will address these questions with our own transcendent biases. But in the absence of federal law on adoption issues, states' laws remain the sole arbiters of these conflicts; state legislatures thus become the last courts of appeal for these adoptees.

News reporting on our time reads, in too many instances, as if we are headed south of the Age of Enlightenment and that our evolution has advanced less than our masquerades suggest. Still, a small step in the affirmation of continued progress toward a more civilized society will ensue when, through informed consciences, state legislators move to draft and approve legislation that will gain for the adult adoptee-petitioner access to his or her original birth and adoption records, with no legal obstacles to that access. *This change in states' adoption laws would render unto adoptees that which is theirs by any civilized standard*, privacy rights and ancient tradition notwithstanding.

| "Many women who give up children for adoption do indeed want to keep their identities secret."

STATES SHOULD NOT OPEN ADOPTION RECORDS

Mona Charen

Many adult adoptees and others advocate reforming state laws to permit greater access to birth and adoption records. In the following viewpoint, Mona Charen opposes one such effort in Ohio. She contends that women who give up their children for adoption often prefer the confidentiality of sealed birth records and that many adoptees do not want their biological parents to seek them out. In addition, Charen argues, an open-records policy would threaten the sanctity and permanence of the adoptive family. Charen is a nationally syndicated columnist.

As you read, consider the following questions:

1. What is the purpose of Ohio's "mutual consent registry," according to Charen?
2. Which specific proposed reforms in Ohio would damage the confidentiality of adoptee birth records, in the author's opinion?
3. What percentage of adopted American children seek out their birth parents, according to Charen?

Mona Charen, "Bad Idea in Adoption Reform," *Conservative Chronicle*, September 27, 1995. Reprinted by permission of Mona Charen and Creators Syndicate.

Certain "reforms," like bad pennies, keep turning up.

In 1995 the state of Ohio was considering a complete overhaul of its adoption laws—ostensibly to remove barriers to adoption. But a great many of the features of the proposed law may have the opposite effect.

Half of the bill's 130 pages deal with the "open records" issue. This is a hot ticket among anti-adoption and "search" groups, which managed to exert pressure on the task force appointed by Ohio Gov. George Voinovich. But advocates of adoption should cast a wary eye on the agenda of these groups. What they are seeking is an end to the decades-old practice of guaranteeing confidentiality in adoptions and thus to the security and permanence of adoptive families. [The Ohio bill was signed into law in March 1996.]

Proposed Reforms

If you ask the average person whether secrecy in adoption should be maintained, he'll probably say no. It sounds un-American. But confidentiality serves important functions in this most sensitive area of human life.

One useful reform Ohio proposed is to provide better information on medical and social histories of babies to their adoptive parents as well as a mechanism for updating such information should that become necessary (for example, when someone in the birth family comes down with a disease with a genetic link).

But opening all records is like capsizing a boat to put out a fire. In fact, the answer to adoptees wanting contact with birth parents (and vice versa) already exists under Ohio law. Ohio currently maintains a mutual consent registry for birth parents and adoptees. If, when an adoptee has reached the age of 21, he wants to contact his birth parents, he can register with the state. If his birth parent or parents have done the same, a meeting can be arranged easily.

Releasing Birth Information

The proposed reform would require that the birth mother, at the time of birth, sign something saying whether she would like her information released to the child when the child reaches the age of 18. Further, unless the adoptee registers with the state by the age of 25 that he does not wish contact with his birth family, his information will be released to his birth parents and/or birth siblings upon request.

How many birth mothers, at the highly emotional time of birth, will say that they do not wish the babies they are giving up to know them? Probably not very many, particularly if the state seems to be pushing them toward contact.

SECRECY IS IMPORTANT

But many women who give up children for adoption do indeed want to keep their identities secret. How is a young woman to know what her circumstances will be in 18 years? Perhaps she will have a completely new family that knows nothing of this child. Perhaps she will be married to a less than understanding husband.

But more than that, the idea of requiring birth mothers to decide whether they want contact or not forwards the damaging idea that adoption can be seen as a temporary matter. Adoption, instead of being the permanent, inviolable formation of a new family, is subtly transformed in the hands of the open-records movement into something different—a temporary arrangement until the birth mother and adoptee are ready to resume their relationship.

THE RIGHT THING TO DO

There are problems with adoption, to be sure—exacerbated by governmental bureaucracy, trendy ideas, and tinges of racism and reverse racism—but studies show that adoption works well for the vast majority of adoptive children, whose welfare should be our first priority. It also works well for most adoptive parents and for birthmothers, who generally grieve for the departed child but are glad that they have given life and are able to get on with their own lives; as one put it, "I knew that something can hurt a lot and still be the right thing to do."

That's not what anti-adoption propagandists would have us believe, though. We are told that adopted children are always searching for their birthmothers—in real life, less than 5 percent do.

Marvin Olasky, *National Review*, June 7, 1993.

Because I have written about adoption frequently (my older son is adopted), I receive a great deal of mail from adoptees and others involved in adoption. Many, many adoptees write of the pain they've experienced when sought after by birth parents they have no wish to see. And birth parents are often put in embarrassing, and sometimes extremely painful, situations by the unexpected and undesired arrival of an adoptee.

Nationally, only about 6 percent of adopted children ever

search for their biological parents. According to data from the Search Institute, adopted children have higher levels of self-esteem than the population at large, are as deeply attached to their parents as are their non-adopted siblings, and tend to be happy.

Finally, consider this: In Great Britain and Australia, open-records laws led to 67 percent and 70 percent drops respectively in the number of adoptions annually. Ohio should tread carefully.

PERIODICAL BIBLIOGRAPHY

The following articles have been selected to supplement the diverse views presented in this chapter. Addresses are provided for periodicals not indexed in the *Readers' Guide to Periodical Literature*, the *Alternative Press Index*, the *Social Sciences Index*, or the *Index to Legal Periodicals and Books*.

Elizabeth Bartholet	"Blood Knots: Adoption, Reproduction, and the Politics of Family," *American Prospect*, Fall 1993.
Kimberly A. Collins	"My Choice Was Pro-Me," *Essence*, March 1994.
Mark Hansen	"Fears of the Heart," *ABA Journal*, November 1994.
Linda Hodges	"Blood Ties," *New York Times*, July 19, 1996.
Steven A. Holmes	"Bitter Racial Dispute Rages over Adoption," *New York Times*, April 13, 1995.
Michele Ingrassia and Karen Springen	"She's Not Baby Jessica Anymore," *Newsweek*, March 21, 1994.
Randall Kennedy and Carol Moseley-Braun	"Interracial Adoption: Is the Multiethnic Placement Act Flawed?" *ABA Journal*, April 1995.
Frederica Mathewes-Green	"Pro-Life Dilemma," *Policy Review*, July/August 1996.
New Republic	"All in the Family," January 24, 1994.
Marvin Olasky	"The War on Adoption," *National Review*, June 7, 1993.
Marlou Russell	"The Lifelong Impact of Adoption," *USA Today*, July 1994.
Julie Shoop	"'Ounce of Prevention' Proposed for Adoption Law," *Trial*, December 1994.
Lena Williams	"Transracial Adoption: The Truth Comes in Shades of Gray," *New York Times*, March 23, 1995.
Naomi Wolf	"Our Bodies, Our Souls," *New Republic*, October 16, 1995.

CHAPTER 5

WHICH VALUES AND POLICIES MOST BENEFIT THE FAMILY?

CHAPTER PREFACE

"Family values"—the principles and morals considered most favorable for the well-being of the traditional family—have become a topic of national debate in the last two decades of the twentieth century. Such contention revolves around a number of issues that affect families—sexual behavior, child welfare, education, and work, to name a few—and is often voiced in the agendas of various political groups and religious organizations.

For example, in May 1995, the politically conservative Christian Coalition unveiled its "Contract With the American Family," a proposal calling for a number of reforms designed to strengthen families, including a constitutional amendment to safeguard religious expression in public places. Pat Robertson, founder of the Christian Coalition, insists that such an amendment is necessary to protect voluntary student-initiated prayer in public schools. According to Robertson, most American families support school prayer; however, he argues, misunderstandings about the separation of church and state have effectively censored religious expression in the classroom. "For more than thirty years, liberals have forbidden little children to pray or read the Bible in schools," Robertson maintains. In his opinion, such a "vendetta against religious values" among educators undermines the country's moral heritage and contributes to the decline of the traditional family.

Opponents of such conservative proposals for the family argue that students have always had the right to engage in individual voluntary prayer. According to Edd Doerr, executive director of Americans for Religious Liberty, state and federal courts have never barred students from praying or reading religious literature: "They may pray silently in school pretty much whenever they please. . . . [They can] form religious clubs. . . . All the courts have prohibited is government-sponsored or -regulated devotions." Furthermore, Doerr maintains, Gallup polls have revealed that 70 percent of Americans prefer "a moment of silence for contemplation or silent prayer" during the school day instead of "spoken prayer." Other critics contend that conservative supporters of school prayer actually want to encourage the growth of religious indoctrination and Bible-based standards throughout American culture. Such an agenda does not genuinely reflect the concerns or the religious, cultural, and political diversity of America's families, these critics argue.

In the following chapter, authors continue this debate about which political and spiritual values offer the best solutions to the problems confronting the nation's families.

| "We should try to strengthen . . . families by private example, public policy, and in any other way we can."

PUBLIC POLICY REFORMS CAN BENEFIT THE FAMILY

Part I: Judith Stacey, Part II: Herbert Stein

The authors of the following two-part viewpoint maintain that government resources and policy reforms can benefit the family. In Part I, Judith Stacey, author of *Brave New Families: Stories of Domestic Upheaval in Late Twentieth-Century America*, contends that espousing the traditional nuclear family as the only viable family form is unrealistic and counterproductive. She argues that policymakers should instead support families through various measures, including health care reform, pay equity for women workers, and government-funded education. In Part II, Herbert Stein maintains that government institutions have a responsibility to the family—particularly to help ensure the welfare of children. Stein is a senior fellow of the American Enterprise Institute for Public Policy Research.

As you read, consider the following questions:

1. According to Stacey, why did Dan Quayle publicly chastise the fictional television sitcom character Murphy Brown?
2. What percentage of America's children in the 1990s are raised in unbroken two-parent families, according to Stacey?
3. In Stein's opinion, what is wrong with the proposed family tax credit of five hundred dollars per child?

Judith Stacey, "The Family Values Fable," National Forum/Phi Kappa Phi Journal, Summer 1995; Herbert Stein, "On Families and Values," Brookings Review, Summer 1995.

One of the stranger spectacles of the 1992 presidential electoral season was the prime-time duel between Dan Quayle and sitcom heroine Murphy Brown. Dan threw the first punch, castigating Murphy for abetting cultural and moral decline by glamorizing unwed motherhood. However, in a moment of supreme irony, anchorwoman Murphy seized control of the match when she took to the sitcom airwaves to chastise the former vice president for being out of touch with the problems of "real" families. Millions of voters watched this well-hyped episode and the televised responses to Murphy's sermon elicited from Quayle and the small group of "real" single mothers he had selected to join him in viewing this electoral spectacle, on camera.

THE FAMILY VALUES BANDWAGON

At the time, most political commentators awarded the forensic trophy to the sitcom single mom, echoing her scorn for the vice president's inability to distinguish virtual from actual families. This failure, which the Republican Party's nominating convention compounded, assisted Bill Clinton's slim margin of victory in 1992. Now, however, Dan Quayle is enjoying the last laugh-in because even President Clinton has since joined the "Dan Quayle Was Right" brigades. Like too many politicians and voters in this right-wing era, Clinton has embraced the misleading ideology of a campaign for "family values" initiated and directed by social scientists who have organized bodies such as the Institute for American Values, the Council on Families in America, the National Fatherhood Initiative, and the Communitarian Network for such purposes. In an article in *The Nation* in 1994, I naively attempted to respond to this campaign by speaking, "truth to power," as student activists used to say, exposing flaws in its selective and distorted reading of social science research about the effects of single parenthood, divorce, and alternative family structures on children. I had not yet appreciated the cultural lesson of the Quayle vs. Brown match. In the age of virtual reality, when the medium is indeed the message, power is truth.

Quayle's campaign against single mothers has scored such a dramatic comeback victory over Clinton, the reputed comeback king, because the former vice president's campaign scriptwriters were quick to grasp the virtual character of contemporary family values. They recognized that Murphy Brown can function symbolically as a wayward stepdaughter of Ozzie and Harriet Nelson, the mythic couple who loom, much larger than life, in collective nostalgia for the world of 1950s families that is currently so rampant.

After all, the 1950s, those halcyon days of the modern nuclear family, were also the years when television became a mass medium, indeed an obligatory new member of the family. From its hallowed living room perch, the magic box broadcast the first generation of domestic sitcoms, emblazoning idealized portraits of middle-class family dynamics into the national unconscious. Because the 1950s were also the first Cold War decade, when the United States became the dominant global superpower, images of an invincible family and nation mingle inextricably in our national imagination of those "good old days." A fable of virtual family values that is currently dominating political discourse in the media-beltway world originated in the 1950s.

A BEDTIME STORY FOR THE AMERICAN CENTURY

Once upon a fabulized time, half a century ago, there was a lucky land where families with names such as Truman and Eisenhower presided over a world of Nelsons, Cleavers, and Rileys. Men and women married, made love, and produced gurgling, Gerber babies (in that proper order). It was a land where, as God and Nature had ordained, men were men and women were ladies. Fathers worked outside the home for pay to support their wives and children, and mothers worked inside the home without pay to support their husbands and to cultivate healthy, industrious, above-average children. Streets and neighborhoods were safe and tidy. This land was the strongest, wealthiest, freest, and fairest in the world. Its virtuous leaders, heroic soldiers, and dazzling technology defended all the freedom-loving people on the planet from an evil empire that had no respect for freedom or families. A source of envy, inspiration, and protection to people everywhere, the leaders and citizens of this blessed land had good reason to feel confident and proud.

And then, as so often happens in fairy tales, evil came to this magical land. Sometime during the mid-1960s, a toxic serpent wriggled its way close to the pretty picket fences guarding those Edenic gardens. One prescient Jeremiah, named Daniel Patrick Moynihan, detected the canny snake and tried to alert his placid countrymen to the dangers of family decline. Making a pilgrimage from Harvard to the White House, he chanted about the ominous signs and consequences of "a tangle of pathology" festering in cities that suburban commuters and their ladies-in-waiting had abandoned for the crabgrass frontier. Promiscuity, unwed motherhood, and fatherless families, he warned, would undermine domestic tranquillity and wreak social havoc. Keening only to the tune of black keys, however, this Pied Piper's song fell flat, inciting displeasure and rebuke.

USING GOVERNMENT FOR THE COMMON GOOD

For the sake of our children, we ought to call an end to false debates between values and policies. Both personal and mutual responsibility are essential, and we should work to strengthen them at all levels of society. Let us admit that some government programs and personnel are efficient and effective, and others are not. Let us acknowledge that when it comes to the treatment of children, some individuals are evil, neglectful, or incompetent, but others are trying to do the best they can against daunting odds and deserve not our contempt but the help only we—through our government—can provide. Let us stop stereotyping government and individuals as absolute villains or absolute saviors, and recognize that each must be part of the solution. Let us use government, as we have in the past, to further the common good. . . .

Government is not something outside us—something irrelevant or even alien to us—but is us. To acknowledge this is to acknowledge that government has a responsibility not only to provide essential services but to bring individuals and communities together. In a democracy, government is not "them" but "us," an endeavor that joins with volunteerism and the efforts of the private sector in sustaining our mutual obligations to our children, families, and communities.

Hillary Rodham Clinton, It Takes a Village, 1996.

It seemed that overnight those spoiled Gerber babies had turned into rebellious, disrespectful youth who spurned authority, tradition, and conformity, and scorned the national wealth, power, and imperial status in which their elders exulted. Rejecting their parents' grey flannel suits and Miss America ideals, as well as their monogamous, nuclear families, they generated a counterculture and a sexual revolution, and they built unruly social movements demanding student rights, free speech, racial justice, peace, and liberation for women and homosexuals. Long-haired, unisex-clad youth smoked dope and marched in demonstrations shouting slogans like, "Question Authority," "Girls Say Yes to Boys Who Say No," "Smash Monogamy," "Black is Beautiful," "Power to the People," "Make Love, Not War," "Sisterhood is Powerful," and "Liberation Now." Far from heeding Moynihan's warning, or joining in his condemnation of "black matriarchs," many young women drew inspiration from such mothers and condemned Moynihan instead for "blaming the victims."

Disrupting families and campuses, the young people confused and divided their parents and teachers, even seducing some foolish elders into emulating their sexual and social experiments. But the thankless arrogance of these privileged youth, their unkempt appearance, provocative antics, and amorality also enraged many, inciting a right-wing, wishful, "moral majority" to form its own backlash social movement to restore family and moral order.

THE "SERPENT" OF FAMILY DECLINE

And so it happened that harmony, prosperity, security, and confidence disappeared from this once, most fortunate land. After decimating African American communities, the serpent of family decline slithered under the picket fences, where it spewed its venom on white, middle-class victims as well. Men no longer knew what it meant to be men, and women had neither time nor inclination to be ladies. Ozzie had trouble finding secure work. He was accused of neglecting, abusing, or oppressing his wife and children. Harriet no longer stayed home with the children. She too worked outside the home for pay, albeit less pay. Ozzie and Harriet sued for divorce. Harriet decided she could choose to have children with or without a marriage certificate, with or without an Ozzie, or perhaps even with a Rozzie. After all, as front-page stories in her morning newspaper informed her, almost daily, "Traditional Family Nearly the Exception, Census Finds."

As the 1990s dawned, only half the children in the land were living with two married parents who had jointly conceived or adopted them. Twice as many children were living in single-parent families as in male breadwinner, female homemaker families. Little wonder few citizens could agree over what would count as a proper family. Little wonder court chroniclers charted the devolution of the modern family system in books with anxious titles such as, The War Over the Family, Embattled Paradise, Disturbing the Nest, Brave New Families, The Way We Never Were, Fatherless America, and Families on the Faultline.

The clairvoyant Daniel Patrick Moynihan found himself vindicated at last, as political candidates from both the ruling parties joined his hymns of praise to Ozzie and Harriet and rebuked the selfish family practices of that rebellious stepchild of the Nelsons, Murphy Brown.

The era of the modern family system had come to an end, and few could feel sanguine about the postmodern family condition that had succeeded it. Unaccustomed to a state of normative instability and definitional crisis, the populace split its behavior from its beliefs. Many who contributed actively to such postmodern family statistics as divorce, remarriage, blended families, single parenthood, joint custody, abortion, domestic partnership, two-career households, and the like still yearned nostalgically for the *Father Knows Best* world they had lost.

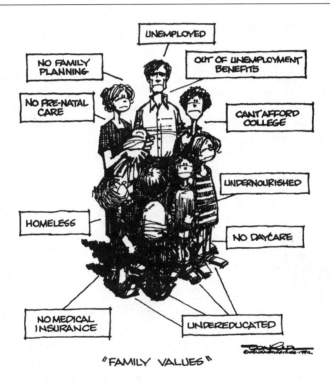

Paul Conrad, ©1992, Los Angeles Times. Reprinted with permission.

"Today," in the United States, as Rutger's historian John Gillis so aptly puts it, "the anticipation and memory of family means more to people than its immediate reality. It is through the families we live by that we achieve the transcendence that compensates for the tensions and frustrations of the families we live with." Not only have the fabled modern families we live by become more compelling than the messy, improvisational, patchwork bonds of postmodern family life, but as my bedtime story hints, because they function as pivotal elements in our distinctive national imagination, these symbolic families are also far more stable than any in which future generations ever dwelled.

Murphy was certainly correct in her claim that this fable of virtual family values is drastically out of synch with the everyday realities and choices that most contemporary families face. What neither she nor I understood, however, is that this dissonance is precisely what augments the fable's emotional appeal, and hence gives it such political force.

In the context of our contemporary social, economic, and political malaise, it is not difficult to understand the public's palpable longing for the world of innocence, safety, confidence, and affluence that Ozzie and Harriet have come to signify. Unfortunately, this nostalgia does little to improve conditions for the beleaguered families we live with, and a great deal to make them even worse. The family-values campaign helped to fuel the Republican rout in November 1994, ensuring the passage of budget-cutting and anti-welfare "reform" measures that will plunge the growing ranks of our least fortunate families, and especially the children whose interests the campaign claims to serve, into ever-greater misery and decay. For apart from exhorting or coercing adults to enter or remain in possibly hostile, even destructive marriages, family-decline critics offer few social proposals to address children's pressing needs. Further stigmatizing the increasing numbers who live in "nontraditional" families will only add to their duress.

We can watch Ozzie and Harriet reruns as long as we like, but we cannot return to the world it evokes, even if we wish to. What we can do, and what I sorely believe we must do instead, is to direct public attention and resources to measures that could mitigate the unnecessarily injurious effects of divorce and single parenthood on the fourth of our nation's children who now suffer these effects. Having surmised that one must fight fables with fables, I offer my personal utopian wish list of such genuinely "pro-family" measures:

- restructure work hours and benefits to suit working parents;
- redistribute work to reduce under- and over-employment;
- enact comparable worth standards of pay equity so that women as well as men can earn a family wage;
- provide universal health, prenatal and child care, sex education, and reproductive rights to make it possible to choose to parent responsibly;
- legalize gay marriage;

- revitalize public education;
- pass and enforce strict gun control laws;
- end the economic inequities of divorce property and income dispositions;
- house the homeless;
- institute a universal national service obligation;
- fund libraries, parks, public broadcasting, and the arts;
- read a fable of democratic family values to the children of the next millennium.

II

O, Family Values, what wonders are performed in your name! In your name some political leaders propose to give a tax credit of $500 per child to every income-tax-paying unit except the very richest. I use the expression "income-tax-paying unit" because no particular family relationship is required. There may be a couple, married or unmarried, or there may be a single taxpayer, male or female, and the children may have a biological relationship to both adults, to one, or to neither. At the same time, also in the name of family values, it is proposed to reduce federal benefits to mother-children units if the mother is young and poor.

America's "Children Problem"

We do not have a family problem in America, or, at least, that is not one of our major problems. We have a children problem. Too many of our children are growing up uncivilized. The family deserves attention today mainly because it is the best institution for civilizing children. We shouldn't get too sentimental about that, however. Through most of history the family that reared children was not our idealized Poppy-Mommy-Kiddies group but a much more inclusive relationship. The first family was the scene of a fratricide. The most famous families in literature, the Montagues and Capulets of William Shakespeare's *Romeo and Juliet*, were obsessed with fighting each other, with fatal consequences for their children. Long before Sigmund Freud we knew that the family could be a nest of vipers.

Despite its blemishes, perhaps exaggerated in literature because they are exceptional, the family is the best institution we know for rearing children. It is the best because it is most likely to be governed by certain values—love, responsibility, voluntary commitment to the welfare of others, including those least able to fend for themselves, who are, of course, the children. That is what family values are.

Government Can Benefit Families

In the rearing of children there is no satisfactory substitute for the well-functioning family. We should try to strengthen such families by private example, public policy, and in any other way we can. But even families that function well need supplementation by other institutions. Some families do not function well, for economic or psychological reasons, and they need even more assistance. In modern societies it is recognized that other institutions have a responsibility and capacity to contribute to the raising of children. These institutions include government, whose wide-ranging functions, from education to preventing child abuse, are generally accepted.

Moreover, there are really no such things as "family values." What we call family values are simply human values that also exist and are desired in relationships outside the family although they are probably less dominant there.

In Support of America's Children

By now, the crisis [of the American family] is painfully apparent to us all. But the solutions that would remedy it are too often ignored, and the means of implementing them are too often withheld. At a time when the well-being of children is under unprecedented threat, the balance of power is weighted heavily against them.

Government has to do its part to reverse the crisis affecting our children, and to do so it cannot retreat from its historic obligations to the poor and vulnerable. Yes, we must work to balance the national budget, but we cannot afford, in the long run—or for much longer in the short run—to balance it on the backs of children. They do not deserve to inherit our debts, but neither should they be denied a fair chance at a standard of living that includes health care, good education, a protected environment, safe streets, and economic opportunity. Children, after all, are citizens too.

Hillary Rodham Clinton, It Takes a Village, 1996.

Our need now is to bring what institutions, resources, and values we can to bear on the problem of our children. From that standpoint the current trend of policy seems perverse. The "child credit" has little to do with the welfare of children. Very few of the children in the tax-paying-units that would receive the credit are part of the children problem in America, or if they are it is not because the after-tax incomes in the units are too small. Little of the income that would be provided would go to the benefit of children. Presumably the additional income would be used for purposes that the taxpayer had previously thought were of lowest priority. Any need of a child that a taxpayer with an income of, say, $60,000 would meet only upon receipt of a tax credit of $500 could not be a very important need. Neither is it reasonable to think that reducing government cash and food benefits to poor children who are themselves the children of poor child-mothers will help to civilize our children, although it may reduce somewhat the number of them born in the future. More care, nurturing, counselling, and education will be needed, in the home, in a foster-home, in a school, perhaps even in an orphanage. The drive to cut costs in the name of family values provides none of that.

VALUING CHILDREN

When I say that "our" children need to be civilized, I do not refer to my biological children and grandchildren, or yours either, dear reader. I refer to America's children. When the bomb exploded in Oklahoma City in 1995 we all wept and prayed for the children. We did not say that they were only their parents' children or Oklahoma's children. They were America's children.

The children growing up in wretched families, in unsafe schools, and in vicious streets are also "our" children. A decent respect for family values calls for more concern with them and more commitment to them than is shown by most of those who now wave the flag of family values.

"To those who say that the solutions to our problems lie somewhere . . . in public policy, I say the reality could not be more different."

PUBLIC POLICY DOES NOT BENEFIT THE FAMILY

Kay C. James

Society should not rely on public policy and government regulations to help solve the problems confronting America's families, argues Kay C. James in the following viewpoint. In her opinion, liberal policies and dependence on government are the root causes of many contemporary societal problems, including the decline of the traditional two-parent family. To rebuild the family, James asserts, Americans must return to a faith in God and a recognition of each individual's personal obligation to home and community. James is a former secretary of the U.S. Department of Health and Human Resources and dean of the Robertson School of Government at Regent University in Virginia Beach, Virginia.

As you read, consider the following questions:

1. In what way is contemporary societal breakdown "a cultural form of AIDS," according to James?
2. According to the author, how have most major American cultural shifts begun?
3. What are the three major points of James's suggested "personal contract with America"?

Excerpted from Kay C. James, "Transforming America," Imprimis, vol. 25, no. 2, February 1996. Reprinted by permission of Imprimis, the monthly publication of Hillsdale College.

An old African proverb has been the mainstay of liberal social science conferences for years: it takes a village to raise a child. Not surprisingly, even First Lady Hillary Clinton is using it in her book entitled It Takes a Village. Its message seems clear: we are all in this together. Three fundamental problems arise with the use of this proverb. First, children do not belong to the village or to the community or to the government. They belong to parents, and the village exists as a resource for these families. Second, even if we did believe this to be true, the village no longer exists. And third, what the village liberals seek to build is, in truth, simply big government.

The proverb summons up a cozy image of all the different segments of society gathering around the innocent babe, protecting it, teaching it, loving it. And as the child grows, the village grows with it. The village is there to guide the child on life's path. The village is there for the child, should the child fall. The village is where all the children will eventually marry and have children of their own, completing a cycle of harmony and knowledge. In trying to name this village, I hope the social scientists considered "Potemkin" because, just as the Soviets used the original Potemkin villages—which were complete shams—to mask the disharmony of their society, this village suffers from incurable dysfunction.

SOCIETAL DISINTEGRATION

It seems that the more our families disintegrate, the more violence explodes in our homes and on our streets, the more our schools fail the grade, the more this old proverb is repeated. Conference after conference, talk after talk, and book after book have discussed the importance of the village in raising children. It is really quite simple, we are told: if only the village would meet its responsibility to its children, all would be well. Children would no longer grow up insecure or worried; they would be well adjusted, well developed, and full of healthy self-esteem. What a wonderful world it would be. . . .

When I was raised, the community supported the family and helped when help was needed. But can we say the same today? Where once neighbors and friends comprised a community, now we are afraid to walk down our own street. Where once the only way to meet the enormous challenges of being black in America meant reliance upon fellow African Americans, today the rate of black-on-black violence has reached epidemic proportions. Previously, families facing hard times could rely upon relatives and friends to help make it; today the sight of homeless men, women, and even children is all too common.

What does this say about our *village?* It says it is gone; that it has been utterly and completely destroyed. Worse, all of the effort and money that has been thrown at our social problems has done little to halt its destruction.

The Problem and the Solution

Ironically, the architect of so much of this failed social experimentation, President Lyndon B. Johnson, recognized both the problem and the solution thirty years ago when he stated:

> The family is the cornerstone of our society. More than any other force, it shapes the attitudes, the hopes, the ambitions, and the values of the child. And when the family collapses it is the children that are usually damaged. When it happens on a massive scale, the community itself is crippled. So, unless we work to strengthen the family, to create conditions under which most parents will stay together, all the rest—schools, playgrounds, public assistance and private concern—will never be enough.

Unfortunately, rather than work to rebuild the *village*, we have instead taken the broken bricks of families, the mortar of cultural institutions, and the steel of houses of worship and used them to build up town hall. Too many of our "leaders" confidently make the claim that where our community has failed, government can and should step in. But reflect upon the state of our community today and you will see what I mean: town hall has been a poor replacement for the institution that makes up a *village*.

Not only is town hall a poor replacement, it has played a major role in destroying the *village*. Dependency upon what government offers—whether empty rights or degrading welfare—has robbed us of the drive so necessary to sustain and strengthen the institutions of the *village*. . . .

Just look to our nation's cities. . . . Liberal theology has undermined our faith and destroyed the traditional role of churches. Liberal education policies have ravaged our public schools. Liberal social policies have sabotaged our families. Liberal public policies have fostered welfare dependency, encouraged promiscuous behavior, and empowered criminals instead of citizens.

Along with the gradual bankrupting of our government, we are witnessing the weakening of our corporate ability to fight off societal infections such as violence, helplessness, hatred, promiscuity, and despair. These "infections" are not new problems, many have been with us for centuries. Proportionally, some may even be less of a problem today than they were one hundred or one thousand years ago. However, our ability to withstand these infections is dramatically reduced by the destruction of the traditional reaffirming institutions of the village. In a sense, we are battling a cultural form of AIDS.

A CULTURAL VIRUS

Just as HIV attacks those parts of the human body that defend against disease, so, too, has this cultural virus attacked what 19th-century French observer Alexis de Tocqueville called the "values-generating" or values-defending institutions of society—the vital components of the village. Steadily, we have seen the most important institutions of society systematically weakened. Individuals, families, communities, churches, and schools are all less healthy than they were ten, fifteen, or thirty years ago. While for all the obvious reasons we certainly do not want to go back thirty years, we do want to keep those things that are good, honest, virtuous, and sustaining. Those things should remain the same yesterday, today, and tomorrow. Those things give us hope and meaning. However, like the "opportunistic infections" that infect the human body, the village is being ravaged by infections that numb the senses—murders, rapes, thefts, rampant promiscuity, and moral relativism. . . .

REAL SOLUTIONS

To those who say that the solutions to our problems lie somewhere in the political arena, somewhere in the economic arena, somewhere in just educating people, somewhere in the crime bill, somewhere in health care reform, or somewhere in public policy, I say the reality could not be more different or more difficult!

The real solutions are not political. The political system is but a subset of the culture and only affects certain areas. It will not fundamentally change this country, or bring it back to where it needs to be. If only it were that simple. We should remember abolitionist Frederick Douglass' admonition that "the life of the nation is secure only while the nation is honest, truthful and virtuous."

Just as the medical researchers of today are seeking ways to build up the cells that prevent infectious diseases from attacking the body, so, too, we must seek to rebuild our social immune system—those cultural institutions that have protected us. That means some pretty tough medicine for all of us. It means that we must be people of virtue. The bottom line is: we need to get out of our easy chairs—love and discipline our children, be involved in our schools, be faithful to the call of God in our lives, be ethical in our businesses, and be involved in our communities. Doing these things is the only way we can reclaim our culture and rebuild our corporate *village* and therefore our country . . . from the inside out.

REFORM REQUIRES EFFORT

When you look back at major cultural shifts and social reforms in our history, they were usually started by one person or a small group of people. Even the birth of this great nation had its roots in a small band of patriots who believed fervently in the everlasting principles of freedom.

The effort needed to rebuild the *village* is not one for the weak or the timid. We are engaged in a life-or-death struggle that will require people who have the spirit of the three hundred men of Gideon—people who will go down to the water and not take their eyes off the battle.

Asay. Reprinted by permission of Chuck Asay and Creators Syndicate.

Pamphleteer of the American Revolution Tom Paine remarked, "When we are planning for posterity, we ought to remember that virtue is not hereditary." The government has not yet invented a program, a piece of legislation, or a department that can give hope to disconnected urban youths, that can help a husband love his wife, that can teach a child honesty and integrity. That is because such a program does not exist. The only place where such an effort can happen is in our homes, and in our communities, and in our churches. Senator Daniel Patrick Moynihan knew this when he said two centuries after Paine, "Government cannot provide values to persons who have none or who have lost those they had. It cannot provide inner peace. It can provide outlets for moral energies, but it cannot create those energies.". . .

THE "AMERICAN EXPERIMENT"

More than two hundred years ago, our Founding Fathers grappled with the idea of federalism as they began what we call today the "American Experiment." While they recognized the necessity of local and even national government, they also desired to create in the new world a system of government that cherishes the individual rights bestowed by our Creator and ensures that government intrusion will be minimized.

In the thirty years since President John F. Kennedy uttered his challenge ["ask not what your country can do for you—ask what you can do for your country"], Americans have not had to consider what they could do for their country, outside of national defense and taxes. Instead, the federal government has told us over and over again what it could do for us. When it told us that it could replace the obligation of families and communities to individuals in need, we accepted this thing called "welfare." When government told us that education should be administered by the federal government and that schools, rather than parents, should teach sexual education and other behavior modification instead of how to read and write and think, we accepted that. And when the government told us that unchecked spending was necessary and that it planned to increase the government's share of every taxpayer's income, we even accepted that.

CULTURAL RENEWAL

Today, we know the full cost of ceding our responsibilities to the federal government. Despite the best intentions of those who created these policies, the government cannot be our parents, cannot teach our children about responsibility and character, cannot regulate individual behavior, and cannot create entrepreneurial opportunities. Education author Charles Sykes calls our government system "the nanny state." I think that "pappy state" is more apt since the government today is raising millions of children at debilitating cost to both the recipients and taxpayers alike because so many fathers neither want to be nor are encouraged to be responsible.

The cultural and political change we are discussing requires two very different yet complementary strategies. While our political leaders in Washington consider redefining the role of government, we must continue to be vigilant in our homes and communities. We must continue to support and work for candidates who share our values; we must voice our opinions on important issues; and we must vote. All these things are necessary and nonnegotiable to transform our nation.

But these are merely actions in the political realm. It is equally important that we develop and carry out a strategy for cultural change. Cultural change must be fought for and won in our homes, in our schools, on Main Street, even in our places of worship. The only reason to rebuild the village is to solidify those nongovernment institutions that support and offer resources to the family. True cultural change will inoculate us when political change threatens our values.

A PERSONAL CONTRACT WITH AMERICA

The challenge today is indeed to ask what we can do for our country, for our communities, and for our families. Instead of waiting for political change to occur in Washington and our state capitals, we must have a personal contract with America—one that renews our individual obligations in a just society. For only by embracing our core beliefs and working for change in each of our lives can we truly see cultural regeneration.

That means that we, not the government, must take care of our neighbors. When it comes to welfare, we are the ones who must give sacrificially of our time and money. Churches will be called upon to become even more relevant to the world in which they exist. In this renewal of self-government, it will once again be individuals of character who will be called upon to lead the way.

A THREEFOLD PLAN

Our personal contract must be threefold. It must also be a corollary to our political contracts. It must begin with our relationship with God, continue in our families, and extend to every institution in our community. In each area, we must take full responsibility and not surrender to the weakness of assigning blame to others.

1. Transforming our relationship with God: in order to bring about change in a sick culture, we must be strong and fortified people—a people who understand both who we are and whose we are. If we are anemic and weak, we will be ineffective, or worse yet, destroyed. We must commit to transforming our rela-

tionship with God through prayer, fasting, fellowship, and study—so that we may be equipped to run the race set before us.

2. Transforming our family: the prophet Nehemiah reminds us to start with individuals and with families. I am convinced that if I saved every "at risk" youth in America and lost one of my own, I would have failed in my primary mission. I am reminded of the old adage that "the family is the original Department of Health, Education and Welfare." You and I must raise children of valor who can distinguish right from wrong, truth from lies, and appreciate the nobility of a life of courage, honesty and integrity. Only in this way can we truly secure the future of this nation.

3. Transforming our community: it is very tempting to seek to save the world while our next-door neighbor is hurting, while homeless people live on our city streets, while a sick friend is struggling to live, or while racist attitudes exist in our community. But if we begin to transform our communities— house by house and street by street—America will eventually become the nation we all desire it to be.

I would be the first to admit that the price of freedom is high. But its rewards cannot be equalled. As Tuskegee Institute founder Booker T. Washington proclaimed in his famous Atlanta Exposition address: "It is time that we embrace freedom and the responsible behavior it demands."

In developing and implementing our renewed social contract, we should remember that cultural change is neither quickly nor easily achieved. In some cases, it can only be measured in generations. But the first steps—rebuilding our families and the cultural institutions of our village—must begin today. And, while the cost is high, the result will be the real transformation of America.

> "We will build ongoing public campaigns to improve the quality of family life by improving the total amount of loving and caring energy in the society."

LIBERAL PRINCIPLES CAN BENEFIT THE FAMILY

Michael Lerner

Michael Lerner is the author of *The Politics of Meaning* as well as the editor and publisher of *Tikkun*, a bimonthly liberal Jewish journal. In the following viewpoint, Lerner maintains that conservatives and the religious right have wrongly blamed liberals, minorities, and the poor for damaging the family, while liberals have largely avoided addressing the family crisis. At the same time, he contends, an underlying need for loving relationships has attracted many people to the pro-family agenda of the religious right. Lerner argues that this agenda does not respect America's diversity and would require adherence to a repressive belief system. As an alternative to such an agenda, he proposes a liberal plan for strengthening the family that recognizes the need for ethical and spiritual values.

As you read, consider the following questions:

1. In Lerner's opinion, what cause of societal selfishness and cynicism do conservatives fail to recognize?
2. How has the world of work damaged family life, in the author's opinion?
3. According to Lerner, what should be the new "bottom line" in America?

From Michael Lerner, "A Meaning-Oriented Contract with American Families." Reprinted, with permission, from TIKKUN MAGAZINE, A BIMONTHLY JEWISH CRITIQUE OF POLITICS, CULTURE, AND SOCIETY (July/August 1995). Subscriptions are $31 per year from TIKKUN, 26 Fell St., San Francisco, CA 94102.

In May 1995, Ralph Reed, the executive director of Pat Robertson's Christian Coalition, unveiled its Contract with the American Family, a surprisingly visionless document that failed to articulate any coherent theory of why American families are in trouble. The family crisis is too serious to be used merely as a Trojan horse to push through Congress a potpourri of unrelated conservative political programs, yet that seems to be the immoral game now being played by the Religious Right.

Let's start by acknowledging what liberals and progressives often miss: There really is a problem with family life in America. Many people are fearful that the family—the only societal institution that explicitly has the task of caring for people regardless of how successful they have been in the competitive market—is now in crisis.

APPLYING MARKET CRITERIA TO PERSONAL LIFE

In a society in which people have learned to see each other as objects, rather than as embodiments of the spirit of God, people increasingly come to feel that everyone is applying market criteria to personal life, always looking for "the best deal," always ready to abandon any given relationship if a better deal (someone more responsive, attractive, interesting, powerful, empathic, younger) suddenly becomes available. The more unsure people are about their "exchange value" on the market, the more they worry about the possibility that their own relationship will fall apart and they will be in a far more difficult position. Unlike the elegant lifestyle liberals who seem to have endless opportunities for new relationships and hence have seemingly little fear of divorce, many Americans feel that their lives would be much worse off if their marriage were to collapse. The freedom of endless opportunities for new relationships that liberals seem to celebrate actually feels to many of the "less elegant" set as endless opportunities for rejection, loneliness, and pain. No wonder they resonate to hate radio and its demeaning of these liberal lifestylers.

When the Christian Coalition speaks about families in crisis, Americans hear that someone is addressing their needs. They may not ever focus on the details of the Contract with the American Family, but they get the message that the Right cares about what is happening to them in their personal lives while the Left only cares about some constitutional principles protecting the rights of individuals to make choices that seem unavailable or remote from the actual lives of the American majority.

The Right points out that the family crisis in America is based on an excess of selfishness, and the Left's excessive focus on individual rights only plays into and strengthens people's desire to put their own individual needs above the needs of any community or any family to which they belong. This inability to commit to a "we," argue some right-wing theorists, forms the rotten core of liberal culture, contributing to the weakening of relationships in general, and to families in particular.

On this last point, the Right is at least partially correct. American society does suffer from an excessive individualism, a narcissistic focus on one's own needs and desires without regard to the needs and desires of others.

But the Right now makes a destructive and hateful move by suggesting that that ethos of selfishness has been caused by special interest groups (African Americans, feminists, gays and lesbians, Jews, immigrants, labor, etc.) using liberal big-government programs to pursue their own selfish needs. And so the Right proposes to dismantle government and put power back into the hands of the states and local governments (often implicitly reminding people of the good old days before the labor movement, the civil-rights movement, and the women's movement were able to use federal power to win rights and protections that they were powerless to win on the local level).

What the Right conveniently fails to notice is the powerful impact of the economic marketplace in fostering a materialistic and cynical worldview, rewarding as wise men those who have been most effective in making a buck, while insisting that sophistication is measured by the amount one can manipulate others for the sake of maximizing one's own wealth and power. It is a worldview that marginalizes love and ridicules spiritual and ethical concerns.

THE NEED FOR MEANING

Yet family life is strongest when it is embedded in a community of meaning (e.g., a religious, national, or political community) that reflects some higher ethical and spiritual purpose. Within such communities, relationships are often focused on how the family might contribute its energies to some higher good, and that higher good, while often connected to the economic survival of the community, usually involves some shared ethical or spiritual values.

When communities of meaning break down, or when they become little more than reflections of the materialistic and individualistic ethos of the market, individual relationships increasingly carry the burden of providing essential meaning. For many, the couple's happiness becomes the meaning of life.

Few individual relationships can fulfil that purpose, and this often leaves people feeling deeply dissatisfied with their families or other loving relationships. They imagine that others are getting their meaning needs met in such relationships and that it is only their own individual failures that have kept them from finding similar satisfaction in their own families.

DEMONIZING THE LEFT

The Religious Right has exploited this pervasive anxiety, correctly telling Americans that it is not their fault that their family life feels jeopardized, that the blame belongs instead to liberals and the allegedly selfish special interests (who are actually the groups who have been most trampled by the selfishness of a racist, sexist, and materialistic competitive market). Many Americans respond with gratitude toward the Right and anger toward these demonized groups.

The Left is unable to respond effectively to all this because the Left doesn't understand that the hunger for love and for meaning and purpose stems from legitimate needs that are being daily frustrated in American society. That's precisely why we need a politics of meaning that can speak to these same needs yet provide a progressive alternative to the Right's analysis.

THE CRISIS IN FAMILIES

From the standpoint of a politics of meaning, a society that rewards people for their selfishness should not be surprised that it faces a crisis in families.

A society that rewards people in the world of work for their ability to manipulate and control others should not be surprised that it has fostered a narcissistic personality incapable of sustaining long-term committed, loving relationships. A society that makes work unfulfilling and alienating, and promotes a meritocratic ideology that encourages people to blame themselves for having this kind of work, will produce people who feel too burned out, depressed, or angry to have a lot of energy for their families.

Any pro-families program that doesn't challenge the many ways that the world of work and the psychic impact of the competitive market have on undermining families is going to be more rhetoric than reality. To be seriously pro-families we must challenge the "bottom line" consciousness fostered by the market, with its privileging of money and power and its implicit message that "looking out for number one" is the goal of life and that caring about others is a concern only for the naive person.

The democratic Left has pointed out that families suffer when they don't have enough economic support, child-care, and health-care benefits. Yet we all know that the crisis in families is as likely to afflict people in affluent suburbs as people in the poverty-stricken inner cities. To the extent that they are unwilling to question how liberal culture might participate in the same excessive individualism and narcissism and materialism that is fostered by the market, liberals will never be in a position to seriously address the breakdown of loving relationships and families.

Positive New Families

Children need warm and mature people around them. We should construct positive new families that meet children's needs, not close our eyes because the world does not fit our icons. We should begin to reach out to one another in new ways, to groups wider than our own nuclear families, and to think of the whole society as part of our family too.

Shere Hite, *The Hite Report on the Family*, 1994.

Moreover, liberals tend to think of "private life" as the sphere in which people ought to seek meaning. Their task is finished, they seem to believe, once they have guaranteed to each individual the opportunity to pursue his or her own path freed from any external imposition. But this picture neglects our deep need for others, and our need to be embedded in a larger framework of meaning and purpose.

A New Bottom Line

The Right seems to be wiser when it notices that our individual lives cannot be complete when we live in a public world that is devoid of larger purpose and meaning. The technocratic and value-free version of public space that was created by the liberal state, complete with impersonal bureaucracies and an injunction to hide one's own real identity in public lest it offend those who are different, is correctly protested by the Right. Yet the Christian Coalition's solution would in effect reimpose Christianity on the public sphere—and that is no solution. Those of us who grew up in a world before Supreme Court decisions protected us from forced recitals of "The Lord's Prayer" and forced participation in Christmas pageants and schools dominated by Christian symbolism have no desire to return to that kind of a world, in which our identities had to be denied in order to be part of public space.

What we need, instead, is something new and complex: a public sphere that is meaning-friendly, but one that does not impose a particular system of meaning. How to build that is precisely one of the tasks we've set for ourselves in the creation of the Foundation for Ethics and Meaning. But we need a way to transform the values of the market, and to create a new bottom line in America, one that rewards institutions and individuals for ethical, spiritual, and ecological sensitivity, one that refuses to grant the title "efficient" or "productive" to institutions that tend to create narcissistic individuals incapable of sustaining loving relationships. . . .

A MEANING-ORIENTED CONTRACT

We do not want government to be the vehicle for the pro-families agenda we propose, and when we talk about families we mean to include single-parent and homosexual families as well. Read our Meaning-Oriented Contract with American Families as a guide to what we need to accomplish in civil society, developed through grass-roots activities, not by the imposition of big government.

1. We promise the American people a campaign to reduce the total selfishness and materialism in society by popularizing a new "bottom line" in America that evaluates productivity of institutions by the degree to which they tend to produce human beings capable of sustaining loving and caring relationships and capable of ethical, spiritual, and ecological awareness and action. We demand of every corporation, governmental agency, and other major societal institutions that they produce a yearly "ethical impact report" that assesses the degree to which their activities, products, and mode of operation tend toward the creation of loving and caring relationships (and we insist that employees of these institutions, together with the public that receives the relevant goods or services, be participants in shaping this report without fear of management reprisals). We seek to publicly honor those who have contributed to the ethical and spiritual life of the community, and those who have dedicated their lives to caring for others.

THE WORLD OF WORK

2. Harnessing the technological advances of the computer age, we advocate reducing the number of working hours for each individual to a thirty-hour work week, redistributing work so that everyone is employed, and thus allowing working people to have more time and energy for family life. More time and en-

ergy for family life may not be sufficient, but it is absolutely necessary to strengthen families.

3. We support voluntary measures increasing employee participation in fundamental decisions in shaping the world of work, thus decreasing the stress that results from powerlessness at work. As workers have less stress to bring home, some of the stresses in family life will be reduced.

4. We support the creation of family-support networks in every community to provide voluntary frameworks of assistance for families dealing with the inevitable tensions in family life. We will create a family-support corps of volunteers in each neighborhood who are available to provide in-home supplemental care for children or the elderly. We will create Councils of Elders in each community and we will struggle to get every societal institution to learn from the accumulated wisdom of our communities' elders. To show that the society values caring activities, we will struggle for higher wages for child-care and health-care personnel, as well as for teachers, family therapists and educators, and others engaged in providing the infrastructure for a much wider framework of voluntary family supports.

PROMOTING SENSITIVITY AND DIVERSITY

5. We support the creation of television programs and networks aimed at providing children's entertainment that avoids excessive violence, rejects the manipulative use of sexuality common on television, challenges the ethos of selfishness and materialism, and focuses on developing ethical, ecological, and spiritual sensitivity.

6. While opposing the creation of any single framework of meaning or purpose, either by the government or in civil society, we encourage a diversity of communities of meaning, and encourage people to understand that their families are strengthened when they are part of these larger communities. Similarly, while people should be free to choose whatever form of family life they wish, we encourage the development of small and medium-sized ethically, spiritually, and/or ecologically oriented communities in which people are validated simply because they are created in the image of God, and without regard to their accomplishments in the marketplace. Such communities will be an important adjunct to family life.

7. We advocate one year of paid "family leave" to ensure that parents are given enough time to be with their children in the first year of life. We also support flexible work schedules so that parents can be home when their children return from school.

8. We advocate changes in school curricula so that every educational system teaches empathy, caring, individual responsibility, discipline, and respect for the experience of others. When parents visit schools to select where they will [send their children], schools must present them with full disclosure not only about the level of academic achievement of previous graduates, but also about the degree to which graduates have shown themselves to embody these values in subsequent years.

9. We seek a society that provides full employment, housing, health care, and child care, but that does so in ways that empower the individual family without the imposition of bureaucratic constraints or a particular lifestyle. So when we have government implementing programs, we want to see more done on the model of the Canadian single-payer plan, less on the model of the bureaucratic monstrosity that was proposed as the Clinton health-care plan.

RADICAL AMAZEMENT

10. We support the creation of public events at which families meet to celebrate and honor as a community the hard work and energy that so many people put into building families, while simultaneously providing a public space (through workshops, small group discussions, educational forums, etc.) to explore the many remaining problems in family life. We will build ongoing public campaigns to improve the quality of family life by improving the total amount of loving and caring energy in the society, by honoring and rewarding those who are best at expressing love and caring in an ethical and spiritually centered way, and by challenging all those societal practices that undermine our ability to see and treat each other as fundamentally deserving of love and caring. And we will encourage people to spend less time in the pursuit of power and wealth, more time in responding to the grandeur of creation with awe, wonder, and radical amazement.

| "Advocates of the new forms of family structure are really advocates of spiritual rebellion against any higher moral authority than themselves."

LIBERAL PRINCIPLES CANNOT BENEFIT THE FAMILY

D. Bruce Lockerbie

Liberal principles that emphasize cultural, religious, and familial diversity do not benefit the family, contends D. Bruce Lockerbie in the following viewpoint. According to Lockerbie, promoters of diversity actually wish to replace America's conventional moral standards with an immoral set of values that would allow abnormal forms of the family to proliferate. Only traditional Judeo-Christian morality, Lockerbie argues, offers the kind of guidance that America needs in facing its family crisis. Lockerbie, an evangelical Christian author and lecturer, originally presented the following viewpoint as one of the Hixson Lectures at Baylor University in Waco, Texas, on February 23, 1993.

As you read, consider the following questions:

1. What is the biblical ideal for the family, according to Lockerbie?
2. In the author's opinion, what is the true agenda of "the Religious Left"?
3. What is solipsism, according to Lockerbie?

Reprinted from D. Bruce Lockerbie, "Merely Players," a paper given at the 1993 Hixson Lectures at Baylor University, Waco, Texas. Reprinted by permission of the author.

It is my great honor to present the first of these Hixson Lectures for 1993. Appropriately here at Baylor University's School of Education and the Center for Christian Education, our theme is "Celebrate the Family.". . .

A family may be defined by the United States Census Bureau as a household, but it is far more than that. A family is a social organism, a dynamic unit whose whole is greater than the sum of its parts but whose *wholeness* depends upon the fidelity and loyalty of its several parts.

The family is a spiritual entity held together not only by bloodline, name, lineage, tradition, address, photo album, or legal documents but primarily by love, pride, recognition, affinity, memory, and responsibility. Physically, a family shares the same genetic code; emotionally, a family may be as disparate as the United Nations.

A family does not spring from nowhere; it is not appointed, like a committee. A family's origins are to be found in the religious and cultural foundations of human society itself. Whatever your understanding of the beginnings of human life, you will no doubt agree that, at some point, man and woman came together for companionship and intimacy, from which relationship—through procreation—a child was conceived and born. Thereafter, that man and woman remained together to nurture that child; so developed the family.

THE BIBLICAL IDEAL

For my part, I am not ashamed to take my stand on the biblical warrants for the family, the biblical ideal: Creation of male and female for the express purpose of loving companionship with each other and with God; for the natural procreation and responsible nurture of children "in the training and instruction [*paideia* and *nouthesia*] of the Lord."

The family is the first and most important influence in the life of every child and every adult. Our parents are our first teachers; our siblings, our first classmates in the schoolhouse called home. Because those earliest roots grow deepest, much of what we learn at home—from parents and other family members—preempts anything else we might subsequently learn from formal schooling or formal worship. So it behooves us all to plant well those seeds that will grow and flourish. And if—as I trust is true—our family life is to experience the knowledge and love of God, then family nurture and admonition will be the earliest form of Christian education.

We are here to "Celebrate the Family." While there is much

within the American family to celebrate, there is also much about which to be justly concerned. Let me list several of these concerns, without expanded comment at this time. Among my concerns are these:

- the disappearance of conventional family norms derived from religiously-based moral principles and their replacement by amoral, if not immoral, alternatives;
- the subsequent displacement of conventional family structure and its mockery by those who justify their chosen alternatives with scorn for that which they reject;
- the effect of experimental medical science upon family norms;
- the still-unacknowledged effect of popular culture's transient values upon family structure and expectations;
- the soaring increase in births to unwed mothers, thereby creating new households typically inadequate to care for themselves and heightening the case, purely on economic grounds, for abortion-on-demand or state-sponsored sterilization;
- the appalling increase in teenage suicide, now the leading cause of death for those between 15 and 19 years of age;
- the increase in family abandonment, whether by husband/fathers or wife/mothers or adult/children of their aged parents;

And this final concern of mine:

- the popular assumption that all such change indicates social progress necessary, if not for the betterment of society, at least for the convenience of our increasingly self-centered manner of living at the end of the 20th century.

HOPE FOR THE WHOLE WORLD

These concerns reveal the principles and presuppositions I bring to this lecture. My concerns, as you can see, are—first of all—religious and moral; then ethical regarding issues medical, economic, legal, and social; then once again, moral and stated in religious terms. You have also recognized the world-and-life view I represent: That of an evangelical Christian, one who sees the landscape of reality through the lens of the Christian gospel, standing on the platform of biblical truth and seeing the world from that vantage and perspective.

Fittingly, at this Christian university, we can expect to speak openly about this Christian gospel—the good news of Jesus Christ—and be understood. That gospel is inherently a word of hope for the whole world. It is not—as Marxists have contended—an imperialist dogma intended to subjugate others; not—as racial separatists have argued—"the white man's religion"; not—as militant feminists have claimed—an oppressive instrument of male domination and repression. The gospel taught by Jesus of Nazareth is liberating, inclusively open to all, wonderful in its power to bring together—out of every tribe and race, every ethos and culture—those who find new life in Christ; for God, who is no respecter of persons, has no favorites.

Strength Through Unity in Christ

But the goal of the gospel is to make us one-in-Christ, not to drive us apart. The goal is to take the resources of our diverse gifts as persons and bring us together for the purpose of creating what St. Paul variously calls God's work of art, God's holy temple, or the body of Christ. Each of Paul's analogies can be achieved only through unity. As the Apostle writes to the Ephesians,—so that the body of Christ may be built up until we all reach unity in the faith—and become mature, attaining to the whole measure of the fullness of Christ. Then we will no longer be infants, tossed back and forth by the waves and blown here and there by every wind of teaching and by the cunning and craftiness of [unbelievers] in their deceitful scheming.

Then Paul drives home his inspired message: Instead of untruth, he calls upon Christians to live in such a manner that by speaking the truth in love, we will in all things grow up into him who is the Head, that is, Christ. From him the whole body, joined and held together by every supporting ligament, grows and builds itself up in love, as each part does its work. Note again that unity is the goal of the gospel, not diversity. Our differences are only the means to achieving strength through unity in Christ; the contribution of each member's gifts is the ideal for attaining maturity, not the glorification of differences for their own sake, which leads only to immaturity and instability.

The Problem with "Diversity"

From such a world-view, I realize, many in our culture—some, no doubt, in this very audience—will recoil, finding my opinions old-fashioned, out-of-date, politically incorrect if not downright chauvinistic; I may be sanctioned for appearing insufficiently attuned to calls for a newly-defined "inclusiveness," "diversity," and "sensitivity" to the far-reaching changes of our post-modern society. I know these critics; what's more, I know what lies behind their criticism. Presumably, they are well-intended and committed to fulfilling their vision of democracy.

But I suggest that their vision is blurred because it starts with the wrong premise and moves inexorably toward a wrong conclusion. As evidence—and rather than citing biblical examples—let me speak about the United States of America.

The historic vision of America is stated succinctly on every dollar bill, in the Latin phrase, E pluribus unum, meaning "Out of many, one." That motto tells why the founders chose to name this nation the United States of America, not the Eclectic or Diversified States. They meant to bring together—under one system of government derived from one common set of moral principles—the vast array of peopless who, by 1776 and 1789, had chosen to make this continent their homeland. The goal of ethnic, religious, and cultural diversity was to be union as a nation under principles attributed to a divine source, "Nature's God," the Creator who had endowed human beings with such "inalienable rights" as "life, liberty, and the pursuit of happiness."

But the current revisionist understanding of American history leaps beyond language, culture, and ethnic distinctives to assert a new kind of diversity. Its proponents are not truly interested in a level playing field for cultural pluralism; echoing T.S. Eliot's [J. Alfred] Prufrock, "That is not it at all/That is not what I meant at all." They demand abandoning the moral framework in which the Declaration of Independence and Constitution were written; they wish to replace the assumptions of Judeo-Christian morality, derived from the Scriptures, with an ethical smorgasbord; they prefer a set of values selectively chosen for the purpose of asserting their right to discard any moral norm and convention incompatible with their own expression of personal license.

The New "Religious Left"

Hear me carefully: The proponents of cultural diversity are not simply advocating the equal validity of all forms of racial, ethnic, or familial expression; rather, they are specifically voicing their opposition to what Henrik Ibsen and George Bernard Shaw also ridiculed as "middle-class morality." These iconoclasts comprise what the writer Fran Leibowitz has recently identified as the new "Religious Left." Let us attempt to understand what she means, for her term exceeds the complexities of identifying one group of Southern Baptists from another.

Religious conservatives have their right wing, often referred to as the "lunatic fringe"; so too religious liberals have their extreme left wing, fanatics like the Lutheran pastor near Pittsburgh some years ago who took it upon himself to purge that city's stately churches and their congregations of an alleged unholy alliance with the old moneyed families named Mellon and Carnegie. So he attacked on Sunday mornings, carrying plastic bags of blood which he broke over the altars and communion tables of what he construed to be those offending churches.

THE GOSPEL OF LIFE

It is above all in raising children that the family fulfills its mission to proclaim the Gospel of life. By word and example, in the daily round of relations and choices, and through concrete actions and signs, parents lead their children to authentic freedom, actualized in the sincere gift of self, and they cultivate in them respect for others, a sense of justice, cordial openness, dialogue, generous service, solidarity and all the other values which help people to live life as a gift. In raising children, Christian parents must be concerned about their children's faith and help them to fulfill the vocation God has given them.

John Paul II, *Origins*, April 6, 1995.

But even beyond such derangement are the leftists who have no recognizable formal religion except the adulation of their pet mania. Insulted by the political gadfly Rush Limbaugh as "environmental whackos" and "feminazis," they are far more than earnest to a fault; they are so caught up in despairing hatred of "the system," they can think only in terms of destroying any semblance of order, conformity, tradition, or hierarchy. Fanatic devotion to animal rights or the rain forest or the evils of the internal combustion engine or male domination in corporate America qualifies them as left-wing fundamentalists, incapable of balance. They become eager martyrs for their cause: the snail darter, the spotted owl, and the next creature on their list of endangered species—which seldom turns out to be the yet-unborn human being.

THE REAL AGENDA IS SEXUAL LICENSE

But the environment and its protection or equal employment rights for women are not the foremost themes for these warriors on the new Religions Left. Most often, the flashpoint that ignites them into flaming combat on behalf of "multi-culturalism" and "pluralism" is reducible to a single three-letter word: *sex*. The fact is that governing authorities in every sphere—political, educational, religious, artistic, entertainment, and now military—are utterly paralyzed by the need to insure that they adhere to politically correct attitudes and responses to sex and sexuality, sex and sexual preference, sex and gender roles, sex and the aborted child.

Whatever the issue may be—cooperative marital infidelity as a swingers' vacation option, laws pertaining to topless dancing as freedom of speech, the AIDS crisis among health caregivers, efforts by transvestites to adopt a child, innovative religious ceremonies to bless same-sex unions, pro- or anti-abortion protests over fetal tissue research, allegations of sexual harassment and date rape, voyeuristic videotapes of students by their teachers, condom-dispensing clinics in our schools, or the rights of the National Man-Boy Love Association to engage in their sexual preference—one can hardly leaf through a metropolitan newspaper or listen to a newscast without being bombarded by opinions and disputes over sex, the kinkier the better.

My point, in short, is this: The campaign for inclusion and diversity and multi-culturalism has nothing to do with expanding the foreign language requirement for a Texas high school diploma or mandatory overseas study for a Baylor degree; nothing to do with seeing the world as a complex of varied societies. Oh, no. What cultural diversity is all about is justifying one's own desire to live by one's own standards—a position called *solipsism*; living in a manner different from what used to be conventional moral norms, living according to one's own pleasures, without regard for moral strictures—especially if derived from the Bible—and denying the existence and authority of moral absolutes. In such a kingdom of the blind, the one-eyed solipsist rules.

Normalizing the Abnormal

Now, to reconnect with our topic: The quest to justify so-called diversity is a political attempt to normalize the abnormal, to legitimatize the illegitimate. Writing in *U.S. News & World Report* [September 14, 1992], John Leo shows how the gender politics of the 1970s and 1980s helped to shape a growing assumption that the conventional two-parent family was inimical to self-fulfillment through economic independence and sexual license. He quotes the sociologists Peter and Brigitte Berger, who in their book *The War over the Family* argue that "the empirical fact of diversity is here quietly translated into a norm of diversity."

To illustrate, simply by reading a newspaper such as the *New York Times* and observing its rhetoric, [one] can get its drift. No doubt you know the controversy in New York City's public schools, where the recently deposed Schools Chancellor Joseph A. Fernandez had attempted to compel an elementary-level curriculum called "Children of the Rainbow." This curriculum includes first-grade lessons featuring the experience of young children who reside with homosexual or lesbian adults, which the curriculum had called "gay and lesbian families." Before being fired, Fernandez had revised that language to refer to "same-gender couples," but book titles such as *Heather Has Two Mommies*, *Daddy's Roommate*, and *Gloria Goes to Gay Pride* still suggest something of the curriculum's slant toward normalization and social acceptance of the homosexual ethos.

Invariably, the *New York Times* refers to the Rainbow curriculum as "intended to teach tolerance of gay families." The *Times* never suggests that the Rainbow course of study might also be intended to coerce taxpayers into accepting instruction at enmity with their moral principles, offensive to citizen-parents who believe homosexuality to be a perverse and essentially genocidal lifestyle. The effect of such slanted journalism is to set up the good guys against the bad guys; the Rainbow curriculum intends tolerance and goodwill, whereas those dissident parents and school boards are assumed to favor "gay-bashing" and bias crimes.

Spiritual Rebellion

In short, advocates of the new forms of family structure are really advocates of spiritual rebellion against any higher moral authority than themselves. While the description they offer for a family intends to accommodate any combination of human beings who choose to cohabit and claim one another's kinship, it matters little what they profess to support—the chaos of surrogate-birthmothers conceiving by artificial insemination for a fee, or homosexual and lesbian partnerships purporting to offer a family environment that is the moral equivalent of loving parents, male and female. I say again, their objection to the definition of family represented by the Judeo-Christian Scriptures is, in fact, an objection to their submitting to any higher moral authority than their own solipsism.

More than "Family Values"

So, now you know the position I represent. But you will also note that I have avoided any reference to the political code-phrase "family values." My choice is far from accidental. While I would surely expect some shallow reporter to identify me as an advocate of conservative "family values," I refuse to allow myself to be dismissed so simply.

In fact, few of us who paid attention to the 1992 Presidential campaign came away with any other feeling than sorrow at the way in which the American family became a political plaything. From radical revisionism in Madison Square Garden to conservative isolationism in the Astrodome, from manipulation on the campaign trail to equivocation in the Congress, from propaganda vendettas waged by fictitious television characters to propaganda assaults waged by ordained ministers of the Gospel, the family and so-called "family values" were caught in a tug-of-war between political self-interest and demagoguish dictates. As a result, "family values" became trivialized into a cliche.

These Hixson Lectures call upon us to "Celebrate the Family," but what is it that we are to celebrate? Certainly, more than "family values." Beyond question, the family as once defined—father and mother and children residing together in love and encouragement—is in a perilous state. Indeed, one author refers to the American family as "the way we never were." Lest we romanticize any concept of family, let me caution you that another author asks, in the title of her book, *Can We Sue Our Parents for Malpractice?* Perhaps we here should ask, Shall we not also grieve for the family?

PERIODICAL BIBLIOGRAPHY

The following articles have been selected to supplement the diverse views presented in this chapter. Addresses are provided for periodicals not indexed in the Readers' Guide to Periodical Literature, the Alternative Press Index, the Social Sciences Index, or the Index to Legal Periodicals and Books.

Barbara R. Bergmann and Heidi I. Hartmann — "A Program to Help Working Parents," Nation, May 1, 1995.

Allan Carlson — "It's Time to Put Families First," Insight, November 29, 1993. Available from 3600 New York Ave. NE, Washington, DC 20002.

Barbara Ehrenreich — "Oh, Those Family Values," Time, July 18, 1994.

Evan Gahr — "Parental-Rights Advocates Push for Constitutional Amendment," Insight, September 9, 1996.

Michael Kinsley — "No, Quayle Was Wrong," Time, May 23, 1994.

Charles Krauthammer — "Down with 'Family Values,'" Time, October 17, 1994.

Albert J. Menendez — "Church, State, and the 1996 Election," Humanist, November/December 1996.

Virginia I. Postrel — "The Children's Hour," Reason, February 1994.

Ralph Reed — "Ideas and Ideals: Let Us Begin the Important Work That Is Ahead," Vital Speeches of the Day, March 1, 1995.

Jack Wertheimer — "Family Values and the Jews," Commentary, January 1994.

James Q. Wilson — "The Family-Values Debate," Commentary, April 1993.

FOR FURTHER DISCUSSION

CHAPTER 1

1. Ralph Segalman and Alfred Himelson argue that liberalism has contributed to the decline of the modern family. Shere Hite contends that democracy has encouraged the growth of healthy new family forms. Compare the opinions presented in these two viewpoints, then formulate your own assessment of the state of the contemporary family.

2. James Q. Wilson argues that single-parent families foster criminality and poverty, while Iris Marion Young maintains that such families have been wrongly blamed for social ills. What evidence does each author present to support his or her argument? Which author's use of evidence do you find more convincing? Explain.

3. Don Feder, George Grant, and Mark A. Horne claim that children raised by homosexual parents are likely to suffer from emotional and social maladjustment. April Martin takes issue with their contention, arguing that children with lesbian or gay parents are as well-adjusted as children with heterosexual parents. Does Martin's viewpoint effectively refute the arguments of Feder, Grant, and Horne? Why or why not?

CHAPTER 2

1. In their respective viewpoints, both Maggie Gallagher and Hanna Rosin discuss evidence of an increase in divorce rates but reach different conclusions. Whose use of evidence do you find more compelling, and why? How might the authors bolster their evidence? Explain.

2. Children have been a primary focus in the debate over the reform of divorce laws. William Galston maintains that no-fault divorce harms children, while Constance Ahron concludes that the harm to children results from the parental conflicts that lead to divorce. Based on the authors' arguments, how harmful do you believe divorce is for families and children? Why?

CHAPTER 3

1. Joseph Bernardin maintains that "family-friendly" company policies help employees to balance work life and family needs. Laurie M. Grossman contends that although these policies are well-intended, they subtly discriminate against childless workers. In each viewpoint, try to find two supporting arguments that you agree with. Why do you agree with them?

2. Eileen Boris and Gwendolyn Mink argue that welfare reform will create more economic burdens for poor families, while Bill Clinton maintains that such reform will enable many families to pull themselves out of poverty. Which viewpoint do you agree with, and why?

3. Mary Monica uses several anecdotes and quotes from interviews to help support her argument that day care harms children. Kristin Droege presents evidence from a number of researchers to back up her contention that day care can benefit children. Which author's technique do you find more compelling? Why?

CHAPTER 4

1. Maria McFadden and Katha Pollitt disagree about the promotion of adoption as an alternative to abortion. Do you believe that policymakers should advocate adoption for women who experience unwanted pregnancies? Why or why not? Support your answer with evidence from the viewpoints.

2. Randall Kennedy contends that society should facilitate transracial adoptions, while Felicia Law maintains that such adoptions may harm minority adoptees' sense of self-esteem. How do the arguments of these two authors reflect differing views on the nature of racism?

3. Mona Charen identifies herself as an adoptive parent. Does this information influence your assessment of her argument against opening adoption records? Explain your answer.

CHAPTER 5

1. Judith Stacey and Herbert Stein maintain that certain kinds of public policy reforms can benefit the family. Kay C. James disagrees, arguing that religious faith and personal commitment offer the best solution to America's family crisis. In your opinion, which of these authors presents a stronger case? Explain your answer, using examples from the viewpoints.

2. The viewpoints in this chapter include several recommendations for strengthening the family. Consider each recommendation and then list arguments for and against each one. Note whether the arguments are based on facts, values, emotions, or other considerations. If you believe a recommendation should not be considered at all, explain why.

ORGANIZATIONS TO CONTACT

The editors have compiled the following list of organizations concerned with the issues debated in this book. The descriptions are derived from materials provided by the organizations. All have publications or information available for interested readers. The list was compiled on the date of publication of the present volume; names, addresses, phone and fax numbers, and e-mail and Internet addresses may change. Be aware that many organizations take several weeks or longer to respond to inquiries, so allow as much time as possible.

Adoptive Families of America (AFA)
2309 Como Ave., St. Paul, MN 55108
(612) 645-9955 • fax: (612) 645-0055
e-mail: llynch@uslink.net • Internet: http://www.adoptivefam.org

AFA serves as an umbrella organization supporting adoptive parents groups. It provides problem-solving assistance and information about the challenges of adoption to members of adoptive and prospective adoptive families. It also seeks to create opportunities for successful adoptive placement and supports the health and welfare of children without permanent homes. AFA publishes the *Guide to Adoption* once a year and the bimonthly magazine *Adoptive Families* (formerly *Ours* magazine).

American Adoption Congress (AAC)
1000 Connecticut Ave. NW, Suite 9, Washington, DC 20036
(202) 483-3399 • fax:(202) 349-1626

The AAC is an educational network and national clearinghouse that promotes openness and honesty in adoption. It advocates adoption reform, including the opening of birth and adoption records. It emphasizes the needs of adult adoptees who are searching for their birth families. The AAC sells books from its book list and publishes the quarterly *Decree*.

American Family Communiversity (AFCO)
542 N. Artesian St., Chicago, IL 60612
phone and fax: (312) 738-2207

AFCO is a multidisciplinary action and education agency engaged in upgrading the various policies, practices, procedures, professions, systems, and institutions affecting the stability and viability of marriage. It publishes the books *Divorce for the Unbroken Marriage* and *Therapeutic Family Law* as well as several monographs.

American Life League (ALL)
PO Box 1350, Stafford, VA 22555
(703) 659-4171 • fax: (703) 659-2586

ALL is a pro-life organization that provides books, pamphlets, and other educational materials to organizations opposed to abortion, euthanasia, and physician-assisted suicide. It publishes booklets, reports, and pamphlets such as *How the I.U.D. and "The Pill" Work: Gambling with Life, Contraception and Abortion: The Deadly Connection, What Is RU-486?* and *What Is Norplant?* as well as the bimonthly magazine *Celebrating Life.*

American Public Welfare Association (APWA)
810 First St. NE, Suite 500, Washington, DC 20002-4267
(202) 682-0100 • fax: (202) 289-6555

APWA is an organization of members of public welfare agencies and other individuals interested in public welfare issues. The association supports state decisions to implement two-year time limits on welfare benefits and favors sufficiently funded federal block grants to states. Its publications include the quarterly tabloid *APWA News* and the quarterly journal *Public Welfare.*

Child Care Action Campaign (CCAC)
330 Seventh Ave., 17th Fl., New York, NY 10001
(212) 239-0138 • fax: (212) 268-6515
e-mail: hn5746@handsnet.org

CCAC is a group of individuals and organizations interested and active in child care. Its purposes are to alert the country to the problems of and need for child care services, analyze existing services and identify gaps, prepare and disseminate information gathered through inquiries, work directly with communities to stimulate the development of local task forces, and bring pressing legislative action or inaction to public attention. CCAC publishes several books, including *An Employer's Guide to Child Care Consultants* and the bimonthly newsletter *The Child Care ActioNews* as well as several resource guides for parents.

The Children's Foundation (CF)
725 15th St. NW, Suite 505, Washington, DC 20005
(202) 347-3300 • fax:(202) 347-3382
e-mail: cfwashdc@aol.com

The Children's Foundation is a national nonprofit organization established in 1969 to promote policies that benefit children and families. The foundation works to increase federal assistance and affordable health and day care for children. Its publications include the quarterlies *CF Child Care Bulletin* and the *Child Support Bulletin* as well as various directories and papers on child care.

Child Welfare League of America (CWLA)
440 First St. NW, Suite 310, Washington, DC 20001
(202) 638-2952 • fax: (202) 638-4004
Internet: http://www.cwla.org

The CWLA, a social welfare organization concerned with setting standards for welfare and human services agencies, works to improve care and services for abused, dependent, or neglected children, youth, and their families. It provides consultation and conducts research on all aspects of adoption. It publishes the bimonthly journal Child Welfare as well as several books, including Child Welfare: A Journal of Policy, Practice, and Program.

Coalition on Human Needs (CHN)
1000 Wisconsin Ave. NW, Washington, DC 20007
(202) 342-0726 • fax: (202) 342-1132

The coalition is an advocacy organization concerned with such issues as education, federal budget and tax policy, health care, housing, and public assistance. It lobbies for adequate federal funding for welfare, Medicaid, and other social services. CHN's publications include How the Poor Would Remedy Poverty and the bimonthly newsletter Insight/Action.

Concerned Women for America (CWA)
370 L'Enfant Promenade SW, Suite 800, Washington, DC 20024
(202) 488-7000 • fax: (202) 488-0806

The CWA is an educational and legal defense foundation that seeks to strengthen the traditional family by promoting Judeo-Christian moral standards. It opposes gay marriage and the granting of additional civil rights protections to gays and lesbians. The CWA publishes the monthly magazine Family Voice and various position papers on gay marriage and other issues.

Families and Work Institute
330 Seventh Ave., New York, NY 10001
(212) 465-2044 • fax: (212) 465-8637
Internet: http://www.familiesandworkinst.org

The institute addresses the changing nature of work and family life by fostering mutually supportive connections among workplaces, families, and communities. It publishes research reports and other information under the headings General Work-Family Issues, Dependent Care Issues, Leave Issues, and International Work-Family Issues.

Family Research Council (FRC)
801 G St. NW, Washington, DC 20001
(202) 393-2100 • fax: (202) 393-2134
Internet: http://www.frc.org

The council is a research, resource, and educational organization that promotes the traditional family, which the council defines as a group of people bound by marriage, blood, or adoption. It opposes gay marriage, adoption rights for homosexual couples, and no-fault divorce. The FRC publishes numerous reports with conservative perspectives on issues affecting the family, including "Free to Be Family" as well as the monthly newsletter Washington Watch and the bimonthly journal Family Policy.

Family Research Institute (FRI)
PO Box 62640, Colorado Springs, CO 80962-0640
(303) 681-3113

The FRI distributes information about family, sexuality, and substance abuse issues. It believes that strengthening marriage would reduce many social problems, including crime, poverty, and sexually transmitted diseases. The institute publishes the bimonthly newsletter *Family Research Report* as well as the position paper "What's Wrong with Gay Marriage?"

Family Research Laboratory (FRL)
University of New Hampshire, 126 Horton Social Science Center
Durham, NH 03824-3586
(603) 862-1888 • fax: (603) 862-1122

Since 1975, the FRL has devoted itself primarily to understanding the causes and consequences of family violence. Through public education, it works to dispel myths about family violence. The laboratory publishes numerous books and articles on violence between men and women, the physical abuse of spouses or cohabitants, marital rape, and verbal aggression. Books available from FRL include *When Battered Women Kill* and *Physical Violence in American Families: Risk Factors and Adaptations to Violence in 8,145 Families.*

Focus on the Family
8605 Explorer Dr., Colorado Springs, CO 80920
(719) 531-3400 • fax: (719) 548-4525

Focus on the Family is a conservative Christian organization that promotes traditional family values and gender roles. Its publications include the monthly magazine *Focus on the Family* and the reports "Setting the Record Straight: What Research Really Says About the Social Consequences of Homosexuality," "No-Fault Fallout: The Grim Aftermath of Modern Divorce Law and How to Change It," "Only a Piece of Paper? The Unquestionable Benefits of Lifelong Marriage," and "'Only a Piece of Paper?' The Social Significance of the Marriage License and the Negative Consequences of Cohabitation."

Gay and Lesbian Parents Coalition International (GLPCI)
PO Box 50360, Washington, DC 20091
(202) 583-8029 • e-mail: glpcinat@ix.netcom.com
Internet: http://www.qrd.org/qrd/www/orgs/glpci/

The GLPCI is a worldwide advocacy and support group that represents more than four million gay and lesbian parents. GLPCI's members believe that the increasing number of families headed by gay and lesbian parents is evidence that the American family has changed drastically. The coalition helps develop support organizations for gay and lesbian families and supports research and education concerning such families. It publishes the quarterly newsletter *GLPCI Network.*

Lambda Legal Defense Fund

666 Broadway, Suite 1200, New York, NY 10012
(212) 995-8585 • fax: (212) 995-2306

Lambda is a public-interest law firm committed to achieving full recognition of the civil rights of lesbians, gay men, and people with HIV/AIDS. The firm addresses a variety of issues, including equal marriage rights, parenting and relationship issues, and domestic-partner benefits. It believes marriage is a basic right and an individual choice. Lambda publishes the quarterly *Lambda Update*, the pamphlet *Freedom to Marry*, and several position papers on same-sex marriage.

National Coalition to End Racism in America's Child Care System

22075 Koths Ave., Taylor, MI 48180
(313) 295-0257

The coalition's goal is to ensure that all children requiring placement outside the home, whether through foster care or adoption, are placed in the earliest available home most qualified to meet the child's needs. It promotes the view that children in foster care should not be moved after initial placement just to match them with foster parents of their own race. The coalition publishes the *Children's Voice* quarterly.

National Council for Adoption (NCFA)

1930 17th St. NW, Washington, DC 20009-6207
(202) 328-1200

Representing volunteer agencies, adoptive parents, adoptees, and birth parents, the NCFA works to protect the institution of adoption and to ensure the confidentiality of all involved in the adoption process. It strives for adoption regulations that will ensure the protection of birth parents, children, and adoptive parents. Its biweekly newsletter, *Memo*, provides updates on state and federal legislative and regulatory changes affecting adoption. It also publishes the *Adoption Fact Book*.

National Council on Family Relations (NCFR)

3989 Central Ave. NE, Suite 550, Minneapolis, MN 55421
(612) 781-9331 • fax: (612) 781-9348
e-mail: ncfr3989@ncfr.com • Internet: http://www.ncfr.com

The council is made up of social workers, clergy, counselors, psychologists, and others who research issues relating to the family in such fields as education, social work, psychology, sociology, home economics, anthropology, and health care. It provides counseling through its Certified Family Life Educators Department. The NCFR publishes several books, audio- and videotapes, and the quarterlies *Journal of Marriage and the Family* and *Family Relations*.

North American Council on Adoptable Children (NACAC)

970 Raymond Ave., Suite 106, St. Paul, MN 55114-1149
(612) 644-3036 • fax: (612) 644-9848

NACAC, an adoption advocacy organization, is composed of members of citizen adoption groups (primarily adoptive parents of "special needs" children) and other individuals from judicial, child welfare, and legislative areas. It advocates the right of every child to a permanent, loving home, provides direct assistance to local and state advocacy efforts, and acts as a clearinghouse for adoption information. NACAC publishes adoption-related materials as well as the quarterly newsletter *Adoptalk*.

Reunite, Inc.

PO Box 694, Reynoldsburg, OH 43068
phone and fax: (614) 861-2584

The organization's objectives are to educate the public on the need for adoption reform, encourage legislative changes, and assist in adoptee, adoptive parent, and birth parent searches when all parties have reached majority. It publishes a brochure, *Reunite*.

Rockford Institute

934 N. Main St., Rockford, IL 61103
(815) 964-5033 • fax: (815) 965-1826

The institute works to return America to Judeo-Christian values and supports traditional families and gender roles for men and women. Its Center on the Family in America studies the evolution of the family and the effects of divorce on society. The institute publishes the newsletter *Main Street Memorandum* and the monthly periodicals *Family in America* and *Chronicles*.

Single Mothers by Choice (SMC)

PO Box 1642, Gracie Square Station, New York, NY 10028
(212) 988-0993

Single Mothers by Choice provides support and information to single women who have chosen or are considering single motherhood. Although not an advocacy group, SMC supports the view that the choice to become a single parent is a legitimate decision. The group has members in nearly every state and Canada who network with one another and share information and resources. It publishes the quarterly newsletter *Single Mothers by Choice* and the book *Single Mothers by Choice: A Guidebook for Single Women Who Are Considering or Have Chosen Motherhood*.

Single Parent Resource Center

141 W. 28th St., Suite 302, New York, NY 10001
(212) 947-0221

The center's goal is to provide single parents with the resources to lead normal family lives and to establish a network of local single-parent groups so that such groups will have a collective political voice. It distributes "Kid-Paks," "Parent-Paks," and the "Tips for Safety" video kits by order form.

BIBLIOGRAPHY OF BOOKS

Henry J. Aaron, Thomas E. Mann, and Timothy Taylor, eds. *Values and Public Policy.* Washington, DC: Brookings Institution, 1994.

Constance Ahrons *The Good Divorce: Keeping Your Family Together When Your Marriage Comes Apart.* New York: HarperCollins, 1994.

Terry Arendel *Fathers and Divorce.* Thousand Oaks, CA: Sage Publications, 1995.

Robert M. Baird and Stuart E. Rosenbaum, eds. *The Ethics of Abortion: Pro-Life vs. Pro-Choice.* Rev. ed. Buffalo: Prometheus Books, 1993.

Rosalind C. Barnett and Caryl Rivers *She Works, He Works: How Two-Income Families Are Happier, Healthier, and Better-Off.* San Francisco: HarperSanFrancisco, 1996.

Elizabeth Bartholet *Family Bonds: Adoption and the Politics of Parenting.* Boston: Houghton Mufflin, 1993.

Gary Bauer *Our Journey Home: What Parents Are Doing to Preserve Family Values.* Nashville: Word Publishing, 1992.

Mary Frances Berry *The Politics of Parenthood: Child Care, Women's Rights, and the Myth of the Good Mother.* New York: Viking, 1993.

Helen Blank *The Welfare Reform Debate: Implications for Child Care.* Washington, DC: Children's Defense Fund, 1996.

David Blankenhorn *Fatherless America: Confronting Our Most Urgent Social Problem.* New York: BasicBooks, 1995.

Angela Bonavoglia, ed. *The Choices We Made: Twenty-five Women and Men Speak Out About Abortion.* New York: Random House, 1991.

Stephanie Coontz *The Way We Never Were: American Families and the Nostalgia Trap.* New York: BasicBooks, 1992.

Faye J. Crosby *Juggling: The Unexpected Advantages of Balancing Career and Home for Women and Their Families.* New York: Free Press, 1993.

Bette J. Dickerson, ed. *African American Single Mothers: Understanding Their Lives and Families.* Newbury Park, CA: Sage Publications, 1994.

William Dunn *The Baby Bust: A Generation Comes of Age.* Ithaca, NY: American Demographics, 1993.

David Elkind *Ties That Stress: The New Family Imbalance.* Cambridge, MA: Harvard University Press, 1994.

William N. Eskridge	*The Case for Same-Sex Marriage: From Sexual Liberty to Civilized Commitment.* New York: Free Press, 1996.
Diane E. Eyer	*Mother-Infant Bonding: A Scientific Fiction.* New Haven, CT: Yale University Press, 1992.
Jerry Falwell	*The New American Family.* Dallas: Word Publishing, 1992.
George Feifer	*Divorce: An Oral Portrait.* New York: New Press, 1995.
Maggie Gallagher	*The Abolition of Marriage: How We Destroy Lasting Love.* Washington, DC: Regnery, 1996.
Irwin Garfinkel, Sara S. McLanahan, and Phillip K. Robins, eds.	*Child Support and Child Well-Being.* Washington, DC: Urban Institute Press, 1995.
Lucia Albino Gilbert	*Two Careers/One Family: The Promise of Gender Equality.* Newbury Park, CA: Sage Publications, 1993.
John R. Gillis	*A World of Their Own Making: Myth, Ritual, and the Quest for Family Values.* New York: BasicBooks, 1996.
Linda Gordon	*Pitied but Not Entitled: Single Mothers and the History of Welfare.* New York: Free Press, 1994.
George Grant and Mark A. Horne	*Legislating Immorality: The Homosexual Movement Comes Out of the Closet.* Franklin, TN: Moody Press and Legacy Communications, 1993.
Robert L. Griswold	*Fatherhood in America: A History.* New York: Basic-Books, 1993.
Sharon Hays	*The Cultural Contradictions of Motherhood.* New Haven, CT: Yale University Press, 1996.
Shere Hite	*The Hite Report on the Family: Growing Up Under Patriarchy.* New York: Grove Press, 1994.
Penny Kaganoff and Susan Spano, eds.	*Women on Divorce: A Bedside Companion.* New York: Harcourt Brace, 1995.
Sheila Kamerman	*Starting Right: How America Neglects Its Youngest Children and What We Can Do About It.* New York: Oxford University Press, 1995.
Patricia Kelley	*Developing Healthy Stepfamilies: Twenty Families Tell Their Stories.* Binghamton, NY: Haworth Press, 1995.
Betty Jean Lifton	*Journey of the Adopted Self: A Quest for Wholeness.* New York: BasicBooks, 1994.
Ruth Macklin	*Surrogates and Other Mothers: The Debates over Assisted Reproduction.* Philadelphia: Temple University Press, 1994.
Kate Maloy and Maggie Jones Patterson	*Birth or Abortion? Private Struggles in a Political World.* New York: Plenum Press, 1992.

Sara McLanahan and Gary Sandefur	*Growing Up with a Single Parent: What Hurts, What Helps.* Cambridge, MA: Harvard University Press, 1994.
Michael J. McManus	*Marriage Savers: Helping Your Friends and Family Avoid Divorce.* Grand Rapids, MI: Zondervan, 1995.
Michael Medved	*Hollywood vs. America: Popular Culture and the War on Traditional Values.* New York: HarperCollins, 1992.
Bonnie J. Miller-McLemore	*Also a Mother: Work and Family as Theological Dilemma.* Nashville: Abingdon Press, 1994.
Gwendolyn Mink	*The Wages of Motherhood: Maternalist Social Policy, Race, and the Political Origins of Women's Inequality in the Welfare State.* Ithaca, NY: Cornell University Press, 1995.
Elizabeth A. Mulroy	*The New Uprooted: Single Mothers in Urban Life.* Westport, CT: Greenwood Press, 1995.
Allen M. Parkman	*No-Fault Divorce: What Went Wrong?* Boulder, CO: Westview Press, 1992.
Valerie Polakov	*Lives on the Edge: Single Mothers and Their Children in the Other America.* Chicago: University of Chicago Press, 1993.
David Popenoe	*Life Without Father: Compelling New Evidence That Fatherhood and Marriage Are Indispensable for the Good of Children and Society.* New York: Free Press, 1996.
David Popenoe, Jean Bethke Elshtain, and David Blankenhorn, eds.	*Promises to Keep: Decline and Renewal of Marriage in America.* Lanham, MD: Rowman & Littlefield, 1996.
Dan Quayle and Diane Medved	*The American Family: Discovering the Values That Make Us Strong.* New York: HarperCollins, 1996.
John A. Robertson	*Children of Choice: Freedom and the New Reproductive Technologies.* Princeton, NJ: Princeton University Press, 1994.
Pat Robertson	*The Turning Tide: The Fall of Liberalism and the Rise of Common Sense.* Dallas: Word Publishing, 1993.
Cheryl Russell	*The Master Trend: How the Baby Boom Generation Is Remaking America.* New York: Plenum, 1993.
Virginia E. Schein	*Working from the Margins: Voices of Mothers in Poverty.* Ithaca, NY: ILR Press, 1995.
Barry J. Seltser and Donald E. Miller	*Homeless Families: The Struggle for Dignity.* Chicago: University of Illinois Press, 1993.
Rita J. Simon, Howard Alstein, and Marygold S. Melli	*The Case for Transracial Adoption.* Washington, DC: American University Press, 1994.
Arlene Skolnick	*Embattled Paradise: The American Family in an Age of Uncertainty.* New York: BasicBooks, 1991.

Benjamin M. Spock

A Better World for Our Children: Rebuilding American Family Values. Bethesda, MD: National Press Books, 1994.

Judith Stacey

Brave New Families: Stories of Domestic Upheaval in Late Twentieth-Century America. New York: BasicBooks, 1990.

Jean Strauss

Birthright: A Guide to Search and Reunion for Adoptees, Birthparents, and Adoptive Parents. New York: Penguin, 1994.

Cal Thomas

The Things That Matter Most. New York: Harper-Collins, 1994.

Elaine Tyler

Barren in the Promised Land: Childless Americans and the Pursuit of Happiness. New York: BasicBooks, 1995.

U.S. Senate Committee on Finance

Teen Parents and Welfare Reform. Washington, DC: Government Printing Office, 1995.

Rick Weissbourd

The Vulnerable Child: What Really Hurts America's Children and What We Can Do About It. Reading, MA: Addison-Wesley, 1996.

Index